Rust Quick Start Guide

The easiest way to learn Rust programming

Daniel Arbuckle

BIRMINGHAM - MUMBAI

Rust Quick Start Guide

Commissioning Editor: Aditi Gour
Acquisition Editor: Siddharth Mandal
Content Development Editor: Smit Carvalho
Technical Editor: Sushmeeta Jena
Copy Editor: Safis Editing
Project Coordinator: Hardik Bhinde
Proofreader: Safis Editing
Indexer: Pratik Shirodkar
Graphics: Alishon Mendonsa
Production Coordinator: Shantanu Zagade

First published: October 2018

Production reference: 2131118

Published by Packt Publishing Ltd.
Livery Place
35 Livery Street
Birmingham
B3 2PB, UK.

ISBN 978-1-78961-670-5

www.packtpub.com

mapt.io

Mapt is an online digital library that gives you full access to over 5,000 books and videos, as well as industry leading tools to help you plan your personal development and advance your career. For more information, please visit our website.

Why subscribe?

- Spend less time learning and more time coding with practical eBooks and Videos from over 4,000 industry professionals

- Improve your learning with Skill Plans built especially for you

- Get a free eBook or video every month

- Mapt is fully searchable

- Copy and paste, print, and bookmark content

Packt.com

Did you know that Packt offers eBook versions of every book published, with PDF and ePub files available? You can upgrade to the eBook version at www.packt.com and as a print book customer, you are entitled to a discount on the eBook copy. Get in touch with us at customercare@packtpub.com for more details.

At www.packt.com, you can also read a collection of free technical articles, sign up for a range of free newsletters, and receive exclusive discounts and offers on Packt books and eBooks.

Contributors

About the author

Daniel Arbuckle is a long-time professional programmer and teacher of programming, and the author of several books on the topic as well. He first started programming on GBASIC on a North Star Advantage running CP/M, but as the PC revolution expanded, his repertoire expanded as well. Daniel loves programming languages, and by the time he'd gotten his PhD in computer science he knew most of the extant languages well.

Rust is one of his favorite of the current crop of programming languages.

About the reviewers

Daniel Durante is an avid motorcyclist, archer, welder, and carpenter whenever he isn't programming. From the age of 12 years old he has been involved with web, system, and embedded programming with PHP, Node.js, Golang, Rust, C++, and C.

He has worked on text-based browser games that have reached over 1 million active players, created bin-packing software for CNC machines, embedded programming with cortex-m and PIC circuits, worked on high-frequency trading applications, and helped contribute to one of the oldest ORMs of Node.js (SequelizeJS).

> *I would like to thank my parents, my brother, my mentors, and friends, who've all put up with my insanity, sitting in front of a computer day in and day out. I would not be here today if it wasn't for their patience, guidance, and love.*

Syed Omar Faruk Towaha has degrees in physics and computer engineering. He is a technologist, a tech speaker, and a physics lover from Shahjalal University of Science and Technology, Sylhet. He has a passion for programming, tech writing, and physics experiments.

His recent work includes *Easy Circuits for Kids*, *Fundamentals of Ruby*, and *How You Should Design Algorithms*. He is an Oracle Certified Professional Developer and is currently involved with a number of projects that serve both physics and computer architecture.

He is the president of one of the largest astronomical organizations (CAM-SUST) in Bangladesh. He volunteers for Mozilla as a representative.

Walt Stoneburner is a software architect, systems designer, and full-stack developer with over 30 years of enterprise-grade commercial application development and consulting experience. He is currently concentrating on concurrency, cloud services, Docker containers, microservice technologies, and web frameworks. He has a background working with search engine technologies, knowledge management, authoring DSLs, designing APIs, and enjoys creating automation processes.

Fringe passions include typography, illustration and layout, user interface design, psychology and social engineering, quality assurance, configuration management, and security. If cornered, he may admit to liking statistics and authoring documentation as well.

Packt is searching for authors like you

If you're interested in becoming an author for Packt, please visit `authors.packtpub.com` and apply today. We have worked with thousands of developers and tech professionals, just like you, to help them share their insight with the global tech community. You can make a general application, apply for a specific hot topic that we are recruiting an author for, or submit your own idea.

Table of Contents

Preface

Rust is system-level programming language with growing popularity. This popularity is driven by its semantics, which encourages the creation of fast, reliable software. In this book, we're going to learn the basics of the language, eventually getting to a point where we can begin writing usable programs.

Who this book is for

This book is for people with an interest in learning the increasingly popular Rust programming language. You do not have to be a programmer already, but it will help if you are.

What this book covers

Chapter 1, *Getting Ready*, teaches how to install Rust and use the supporting tools **cargo** and **rustup**.

Chapter 2, *Basics of the Rust Language*, teaches the basic language syntax and fundamental semantic constructs.

Chapter 3, *The Big Ideas – Ownership and Borrowing*, discusses the things that set Rust apart from other programming languages.

Chapter 4, *Making Decisions by Pattern Matching*, explains how to use `if let` and `match` expressions.

Chapter 5, *One Date Type Representing Multiple Kinds of Data*, covers enumerations and trait objects.

Chapter 6, *Heap Memory and Smart Pointers*, explores the `Box`, `Rc`, `RefCell`, `Arc`, `Mutex`, and `RwLock` smart pointers.

Chapter 7, *Generic Types*, explains how to use generic type parameters with our data types.

Chapter 8, *Important Standard Traits*, covers traits that integrate with the language syntax and affect the behavior of the compiler.

To get the most out of this book

At least some familiarity with another programming language will be helpful, for comparison and contrast. You will need an internet connection to download and install the compiler toolchain. The ability to use command-line tools is assumed.

Download the example code files

You can download the example code files for this book from your account at www.packt.com. If you purchased this book elsewhere, you can visit www.packt.com/support and register to have the files emailed directly to you.

You can download the code files by following these steps:

1. Log in or register at www.packt.com.
2. Select the **SUPPORT** tab.
3. Click on **Code Downloads & Errata**.
4. Enter the name of the book in the **Search** box and follow the onscreen instructions.

Once the file is downloaded, please make sure that you unzip or extract the folder using the latest version of:

- WinRAR/7-Zip for Windows
- Zipeg/iZip/UnRarX for Mac
- 7-Zip/PeaZip for Linux

The code bundle for the book is also hosted on GitHub at https://github.com/PacktPublishing/Rust-Quick-Start-Guide. In case there's an update to the code, it will be updated on the existing GitHub repository.

We also have other code bundles from our rich catalog of books and videos available at https://github.com/PacktPublishing/. Check them out!

Download the color images

We also provide a PDF file that has color images of the screenshots/diagrams used in this book. You can download it here: https://www.packtpub.com/sites/default/files/downloads/9781789616705_ColorImages.pdf.

Conventions used

There are a number of text conventions used throughout this book.

`CodeInText`: Indicates code words in text, database table names, folder names, filenames, file extensions, pathnames, dummy URLs, user input, and Twitter handles. Here is an example: "Mount the downloaded `WebStorm-10*.dmg` disk image file as another disk in your system."

A block of code is set as follows:

```
fn main() {
    println!("Hello, world!");
}
```

When we wish to draw your attention to a particular part of a code block, the relevant lines or items are set in bold:

```
if 3 > 4 {
    println!("Uh-oh. Three is greater than four.");
}
else if 3 == 4 {
    println!("There seems to be something wrong with math.");
}
```

Any command-line input or output is written as follows:

```
$ mkdir css
$ cd css
```

Bold: Indicates a new term, an important word, or words that you see onscreen. For example, words in menus or dialog boxes appear in the text like this. Here is an example: "Select **System info** from the **Administration** panel."

Warnings or important notes appear like this.

Tips and tricks appear like this.

Get in touch

Feedback from our readers is always welcome.

General feedback: If you have questions about any aspect of this book, mention the book title in the subject of your message and email us at customercare@packtpub.com.

Errata: Although we have taken every care to ensure the accuracy of our content, mistakes do happen. If you have found a mistake in this book, we would be grateful if you would report this to us. Please visit www.packt.com/submit-errata, selecting your book, clicking on the Errata Submission Form link, and entering the details.

Piracy: If you come across any illegal copies of our works in any form on the Internet, we would be grateful if you would provide us with the location address or website name. Please contact us at copyright@packt.com with a link to the material.

If you are interested in becoming an author: If there is a topic that you have expertise in and you are interested in either writing or contributing to a book, please visit authors.packtpub.com.

Reviews

Please leave a review. Once you have read and used this book, why not leave a review on the site that you purchased it from? Potential readers can then see and use your unbiased opinion to make purchase decisions, we at Packt can understand what you think about our products, and our authors can see your feedback on their book. Thank you!

For more information about Packt, please visit packt.com.

Getting Ready 1

In this guide, we're going to learn the basics of working with Rust, a systems-level programming language that has been making a name for itself over the last few years. Rust is a strict language, designed to make the most common errors impossible and less common errors obvious.

Being a systems-level language means that Rust is guided by the needs of low-level programs that don't have a safety net, because they *are* the safety net for higher-level programs. Operating system kernels, web browsers, and other critical pieces of infrastructure are systems-level applications.

This is not to say that Rust can only be used for writing critical infrastructure, of course. The efficiency and reliability of Rust code can benefit any program. It's just that the priorities for higher-level code can be different.

In this chapter, we're going to cover the following topics:

- The `rustup` tool
- The `cargo` tool
- How to start a new Rust project
- How to compile a Rust project
- How to locate third-party libraries
- How to manage dependencies
- How to keep a Rust installation up-to-date
- How to switch between stable and beta Rust

Installing Rust

Installing Rust on any supported platform is simple. All we need to do is navigate to `https://rustup.rs/`. That page will give us a single-step procedure to install the command-line Rust compiler. The procedure differs slightly depending on the platform, but it's never difficult. Here we see the `rustup.rs` page for Linux:

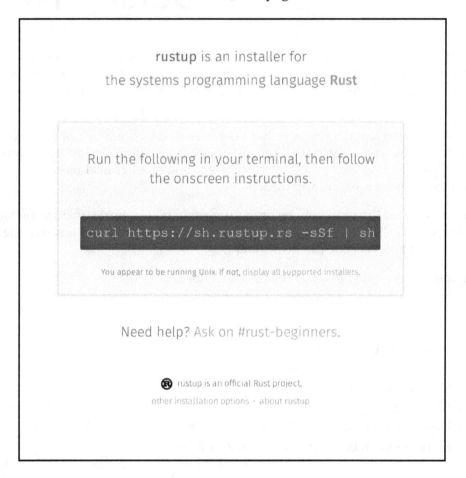

The installer doesn't just install the Rust compiler, it also installs a tool called `rustup` that can be used at any time to upgrade our compiler to the latest version. To do this, all we have to do is open up a command-line (or Terminal) window, and type: `rustup update`.

Upgrading the compiler needs to be simple because the Rust project uses a six-week rapid release schedule, meaning there's a new version of the compiler every six weeks, like clockwork. Each release contains whatever new features have been deemed to be stable in the six weeks since the previous release, in addition to the features of previous releases.

 Don't worry, the rapid release of new features doesn't mean that those features were slapped together in the six weeks prior to the release. It's common for them to have spent years in development and testing prior to that. The release schedule just makes sure that, once a feature is deemed to be truly stable, it doesn't take long to get into our hands.

If we aren't willing to wait for a feature to be vetted and stabilized, for whatever reason, we can also use `rustup` to download, install, and update the *beta* or *nightly* releases of the compiler.

To download and install the beta compiler, we just need to type this: `rustup toolchain install beta`.

From that point on, when we use `rustup` to update our compiler, it will make sure that we have the newest versions of both the stable and beta compilers. We can then make the beta compiler active with `rustup default beta`.

Please note that the beta compiler is not the same thing as the next release of the stable compiler. The beta version is where features live before they graduate to stable, and features can and do remain in beta for years.

The nightly version is at most 24 hours behind the development code repository, which means that it might be broken in any number of ways. It's not particularly useful unless you're actually participating in the development of Rust itself. However, should you want to try it out, `rustup` can install and update it as well. You might also find yourself depending on a library that someone else has written that depends on features that only exist in the nightly build, in which case you'll need to tell `rustup` that you need the nightly build, too.

One of the things `rustup` will install is a tool called `cargo`, which we'll be seeing a lot of in this chapter, and using behind the scenes for the rest of this book. The `cargo` tool is the frontend to the whole Rust compiler system: it is used for creating new Rust project directories containing the initial boilerplate code for a program or library, for installing and managing dependencies, and for compiling Rust programs, among other things.

Starting a new project

Okay, so we've installed the compiler. Yay! But how do we use it?

The first step is to open up a command-line window, and navigate to the directory where we want to store our new project. Then we can create the skeleton of a new program with `cargo new foo`.

When we do this, `cargo` will create a new directory named `foo` and set up the skeletal program inside it.

The default is for `cargo` to create the skeleton of an executable program, but we can also tell it to set up a new library for us. All that takes is an additional command-line argument (`bar` is the name of the new directory that will be created, like `foo`): `cargo new --lib bar`.

When we look inside the newly created `foo` directory, we see a file called `Cargo.toml` and a sub-directory called `src`. There may also be a Git version control repository, which we will ignore for now.

Project metadata

The `Cargo.toml` file is where metadata about the program is stored. That includes the program's name, version number, and authors, but importantly it also has a section for dependencies. Editing the content of the `[dependencies]` section is how we tell Rust that our code should be linked to external libraries when it is compiled, which libraries and versions to use, and where to find them. External libraries are collections of source code that were packaged up in order to make them easy to use as components of other programs. By finding and linking good libraries, we can save the time and effort of writing our whole program ourselves. Instead, we can write only the part that nobody else has already done.

 By the way, `.toml` files are written in **Tom's Obvious, Minimal Language** (TOML), a more well-defined and feature-complete version of the old `.ini` format that Microsoft popularized but never standardized. TOML is becoming quite popular, and is supported and used in a wide variety of languages and applications. You can find the language specification at `https://github.com/toml-lang/toml`.

Dependencies on libraries from crates.io

If a library that our program depends on is published on `https://crates.io/`, all we have to do to link it is add its linking code to the dependencies section. Let's say we want to use **serde** (a tool for turning Rust data into formats such as JSON and back) in our program. First, we find its linking code with: `cargo search serde`.

 I originally found out about **serde** by browsing through `crates.io`, an exploration that I would encourage you to try as well.

This will print out a list of matches that looks something like this:

```
    serde = "1.0.70"                         # A generic
serialization/deserialization framework
    serde_json = "1.0.24"                    # A JSON serialization file
format
    serde_derive_internals = "0.23.1"      # AST representation used by
Serde derive macros. Unstable.
    serde_any = "0.5.0"                      # Dynamic serialization and
deserialization with the format chosen at runtime
    serde_yaml = "0.7.5"                     # YAML support for Serde
    serde_bytes = "0.10.4"                   # Optimized handling of `&[u8]`
and `Vec<u8>` for Serde
    serde_traitobject = "0.1.0"        # Serializable trait objects.  This
library enables the serialization of trait objects such...
    cargo-ssearch = "0.1.2"                  # cargo-ssearch: cargo search on
steroids
    serde_codegen_internals = "0.14.2"     # AST representation used by
Serde codegen. Unstable.
    serde_millis = "0.1.1"                   #     A serde wrapper that
stores integer millisecond value for timestamps     and duration...
    ... and 458 crates more (use --limit N to see more)
```

The first one is the core `serde` library, and the linking code is the part of the line before the # symbol. All we have to do is copy and paste that into the dependencies section of `Cargo.toml`, and Rust will know that it should compile and link `serde` when it compiles our `foo` program. So, the dependencies section of `Cargo.toml` would look like this:

```
[dependencies]
serde = "1.0.70"
```

Dependencies on Git repositories

Depending on a library stored in the Git version control system, either locally or remotely, is also easy. The linking code is slightly different, but it looks like this:

```
[dependencies]
thing = { git = "https://github.com/example/thing" }
```

We tell Rust where to find the repository, and it knows how to check it out, compile it, and link it with our program. The repository location doesn't have to be a URL; it can be any repository location that the git command recognizes.

Dependencies on local libraries

We can also link against other libraries stored on our own systems, of course. To do this, we just have to add an entry such as this to our Cargo.toml file:

```
[dependencies]
example = { path = "/path/to/example" }
```

The path can be absolute or relative. If it's relative, it's interpreted as being relative to the directory containing our Cargo.toml file.

Automatically generated source files

When creating an executable program, cargo adds a file called main.rs to our project as it is created. For a newly created library, it instead adds lib.rs. In either case, that file is the entry point for the whole project.

Let's take a look at the boilerplate main.rs file:

```
fn main() {
    println!("Hello, world!");
}
```

Simple enough, right? Cargo's default program is a Rust version of the classic `hello world` program, which has been re-implemented countless times by new programmers in every conceivable programming language.

If we look at a new library's `lib.rs` file, things are a little more interesting:

```
#[cfg(test)]
mod tests {
    #[test]
    fn it_works() {
        assert_eq!(2 + 2, 4);
    }
}
```

Instead of having a main function, which all executable programs need because they need a place to start, the library boilerplate includes a framework for automated tests and a single test that confirms that 2 + 2 = 4.

Compiling our project

The basic command to compile a Rust program is simple: `cargo build`.

We need to be in the directory containing `Cargo.toml` (or any subdirectory of that directory) in order to be able to do this, since that's how the `cargo` program knows which project to compile. However, we don't need to give it any other information, since everything it needs to know is in the metadata file.

Here, we see the result of building the `chapter02` source code:

```
$ cargo build
    Compiling chapter02 v0.1.0 (file:///home/djarb/writing/RustQSG/Rust-Quick-Start-Guide/chapter02)
warning: unused variable: `cons_invalid`
  --> src/structs_and_behavior.rs:65:13
   |
65 |        let mut cons_invalid = new_constrained(100, 0, 0)?;
   |                ^^^^^^^^^^^^ help: consider using `_cons_invalid` instead
   |
   = note: #[warn(unused_variables)] on by default

warning: variable does not need to be mutable
  --> src/structs_and_behavior.rs:65:9
   |
65 |        let mut cons_invalid = new_constrained(100, 0, 0)?;
   |            ----^^^^^^^^^^^^
   |            |
   |            help: remove this `mut`
   |
   = note: #[warn(unused_mut)] on by default

warning: unused arithmetic operation which must be used
  --> src/expressions.rs:54:37
   |
54 |        println!("Block result {:?}", { 2 + 2; 19 % 3; println!("In a block"); true});
   |                                                ^^^^^^
   |
   = note: #[warn(unused_must_use)] on by default

warning: unused arithmetic operation which must be used
  --> src/expressions.rs:54:44
   |
54 |        println!("Block result {:?}", { 2 + 2; 19 % 3; println!("In a block"); true});
   |                                                ^^^^^^
   |
    Finished dev [unoptimized + debuginfo] target(s) in 4.51s
$ 
```

The warnings are expected and do not prevent the compile from succeeding. If we look at those warnings carefully, we can see that Rust is a lot more helpful with its warnings than many programming languages, giving us hints for improving efficiency and such, rather than just talking about language syntax.

When we build the program, a `Cargo.lock` file and `target` directory are created.

`Cargo.lock` records the exact versions of dependencies that were used to build the project, which makes it much easier to produce repeatable results from different compilations of the same program. It's largely safe to ignore this file, as `cargo` will usually take care of anything that needs to be done with it.

The Rust community recommends that the `Cargo.lock` file should be added to your version control system (Git, for example) if your project is a program, but not if your project is a library. That's because a program's `Cargo.lock` file stores all of the versions that resulted in a successful compile of a complete program, where a library's only encompasses part of the picture, and so can lead to more confusion than help when distributed to others.

The `target` directory contains all of the build artifacts and intermediate files resulting from the compilation process, as well as the final program file. Storing the intermediate files allows future compiles to process only those files that need to be processed, and so speeds up the compilation process.

Our program itself is in the `target/debug/foo` file (or `target\debug\foo.exe` on Windows) and we can navigate to it and run it manually if we want to. However, `cargo` provides a shortcut: `cargo run`.

We can use that command from any subdirectory of our project, and it will find and run our program for us.

Additionally, `cargo run` implies `cargo build`, meaning that if we've changed the source code since the last time we ran the program, `cargo run` will recompile the program before running it. That means we can just alternate between making changes to our code and executing it with `cargo run` to see it in action.

Debug and release builds

You may have noticed that the program was in a directory called `target/debug`. What's that about? By default, `cargo` builds our program in debug mode, which is what a programmer normally wants.

That means that the resulting program is instrumented to work with the `rust-gdb` debugging program so we can examine what is happening in its internals, and to provide useful information in crash dumps and such, as well as skipping the compiler's optimization phase. The optimizations are skipped because they rearrange things in such a way that it makes debugging information almost incomprehensible.

However, sometimes a program doesn't have any more bugs (that we know about) and we're ready to ship it out to others. To construct our final, optimized version of the program, we use `cargo build --release`.

This will construct the release version of the program, and leave it in `target/release/foo`. We can copy it from there and package it up for distribution.

Dynamic libraries, software distribution, and Rust

For the most part, Rust avoids using dynamic libraries. Instead, all of the dependencies of a Rust program are linked directly into the executable, and only select operating system libraries are dynamically linked. This makes Rust programs a little larger than you might expect, but a few megabytes are of no concern in the era of gigabytes. In exchange, Rust programs are very portable and immune to dynamically linked library version issues.

That means that, if a Rust program works at all, it's going to work on pretty much any computer running roughly the same operating system and architecture it was compiled for, with no hassles. You can take your release version of a Rust program, zip it up, and email it to someone else with confidence that they will have no problem running it.

This doesn't entirely eliminate external dependencies. If your program is a client, the server it connects to needs to be available, for example. However, it does greatly simplify the whole packaging and distribution process.

Using crates.io

We saw `cargo search` earlier, which allowed us a quick and easy way to find third-party libraries from the command line, so that we could link them with our own program. That's very useful, but sometimes we want a little more information than what that provides. It's really most useful when we know exactly which library we want and just need a quick reference to the linking code.

When we *don't* know exactly what we want, it's usually better to use a web browser to look around `https://crates.io/` and find options.

When we find an interesting or useful library in the web browser, we get the following:

- The linking code
- Introductory information
- Documentation
- Popularity statistics
- Version history
- License information
- A link to the library's web site
- A link to the source code

This richer information is useful for figuring out which library or libraries are best suited to our projects. Picking the best libraries for the job saves a lot of time in the end, so the web interface to `crates.io` is great.

The front page of `crates.io` shows new and popular libraries, divided up in several ways, and these can be interesting and useful to explore. However, the main value is the search box. Using the search box, we can usually find several candidates for any library needs we may have.

Summary

So, now we know how to install the Rust compiler, set up a Rust project, find and link useful third-party libraries, and compile source code into a usable program. We've also taken a basic look at the boilerplate code that `cargo` generates when we ask it to set up a new program or library project for us. We've learned about the difference between a debugging build and a release build and taken a quick look at what's involved in distributing a Rust program to users.

Coming up in `Chapter 2`, *Basics of the Rust Language*, we're going to begin looking at the Rust programming language itself, rather than the support facilities that surround it. We're going to see how the language is structured and some of the most important commands.

Basics of the Rust Language

2

Okay, we're ready to actually begin writing some Rust code. In this chapter, we're going to look at how Rust programs are structured, and how an assortment of common programming elements are expressed in the language. We'll start with functions and modules, then move on to fundamental language features, such as branching, looping, and data structures. Almost everything we're covering in this chapter has an equivalent in most other programming languages; these are the fundamentals of programming.

Specifically, this chapter describes the following:

- Functions, which are somewhat like miniature programs that are part of the larger program
- Modules, which are used to organize the program
- Expressions, which are how we tell the program to actually do specific things
- Branching, which is how we tell the program to make a decision
- Looping, which is how we tell the program to perform extended actions
- Structures, which is how we organize information for the program to process
- Attaching functions to structures or other data types, to make them more useful

Functions

We saw a couple of functions, in passing, in the last chapter when we looked at the automatically generated boilerplate code created by `cargo new`. What were we actually seeing, though?

A **function** is a sequence of instructions for the computer to follow. It's sort of like a recipe. We don't have to tell a person how much flour, sugar, and milk to use to bake cookies, if we know that they already have a cookie recipe. We can just say: *Bake some cookies, please*. It's similar with a function. We don't have to tell the computer exactly how to save some information to a database; if there's a `save_to_database` function, we can use it to do the job.

In Rust, instructions that can tell the computer to take action can *only* be written inside of functions. It all starts with a function called `main`, which can cause other functions to run, which can in turn cause yet more functions to run, and so on. Using our recipe analogy again, it's like a pie recipe saying: *Use the recipe on page 57 to make dough for the crust.*

Defining a function

In Rust, a function starts off with the `fn` keyword. A keyword is a sequence of letters or symbols which has a fixed meaning in the language. Nothing we do in our program can change the meaning of a keyword, and the libraries we use can't change the meaning either. Keywords occasionally have different meaning in clearly different contexts, but they always mean the same thing when used in the same way. Keywords are the solid foundation that everything else is built on.

So, the `fn` keyword is used to tell the Rust compiler that we're about to tell it about a new function. After that, separated by a space, comes the function's name. There are rules for what the function name can look like:

- It must be made up of the following:
    - English letters (the letters `A` through `Z`, in their lowercase or CAPITAL forms)
    - Arabic numerals (the digits `0` through `9`)
    - Underscores(_)
- It can't start with a number (so `7samurai` is not a valid name)
- If it starts with an underscore, it must have at least one further character (_ by itself has a special meaning)

Then comes an open parenthesis `(` and a close parenthesis `)`, with a list of parameters between them. We're going to gloss over the parameter list for now and come back to that later. There doesn't have to be anything between the parenthesis if the function does not need parameters, and that's how we'll do it for now.

After the close parenthesis of the parameter list, we can optionally include a → symbol followed by a return type, another thing which we'll go into in more detail later.

Next comes a { symbol, which tells Rust that we're about to begin a sequence of commands, followed by as many commands as we need in order to tell Rust how to do what we want the function to do, and then finally a } symbol to mark the end.

Going back to the boilerplate code, Let's take a look at the automatically generated `main` function again:

```
fn main() {
    println!("Hello, world!");
}
```

Here, we can see the `fn` keyword, function name, and empty parameter list. The optional return type has been omitted. Then, between the { and }, we see a single instruction, which tells the computer that we want it to print out **Hello, world!** whenever we tell it to run the `main` function.

There's not a lot more to say about functions until we have some understanding of what kinds of instructions we can give the computer, between those { and } symbols. The main idea is that we can bundle up many instructions into a function, and then use a single instruction elsewhere in the program to tell the computer *to do all that stuff*.

Modules

Modules give us a way to organize our functions (and other items that have names, such as data structures) into categories. This helps us keep things organized, and allows us to use the same name more than once, as long as we only use it once per module. It also lets us use shorter versions of a thing's name most of the time, but gives us a longer version we can use when those short names might be confusing or ambiguous.

Defining a module

Defining a module is easy. In any `.rs` file which the compiler is going to be looking at, we can use the `mod` keyword to start a new module. There are two different ways to use that keyword, though, depending on whether we want to define the module as a section of the current file or as a separate file.

A module as a section of a file

To define a module as a section of a file, we use the mod keyword followed by a name and then a { symbol, then the contents of the module, and then a } symbol to finish it up.

So, if we define a new module containing a couple of functions, it would look something like this:

```
pub mod module_a {
    pub fn a_thing() {
        println!("This is a thing");
    }
    pub fn a_second_thing() {
        a_thing();
        println!("This is another thing");
    }
}
```

We've created a module named module_a and put the a_thing and a_second_thing functions inside of it. We haven't seen it previously, but the line in a_second_thing that says a_thing(); is an instruction to the computer to run the a_thing function. So, when a_second_thing runs, the first thing it does is run a_thing, and then it prints out its own message afterwards.

 The pub keyword means that module_a is part of the public interface of the current module, rather than just being internal data. We'll talk more about that soon.

A module as a separate file

More often than not, we're going to want to give our modules their own files. It's just nicer to keep things separated and contained as much as possible, because it helps keep the code manageable. Fortunately, this is just as easy. In our .rs file, we can just write something like the following:

```
pub mod module_b;
```

That looks a lot like the previous example, except that it doesn't have the module contents right there between { and }. Instead, the Rust compiler goes looking for a file called either `module_b.rs` or `module_b/mod.rs`, and uses the whole file as the contents of the `module_b` module. So, if the file contains a couple of functions similar to the ones we saw previously:

```
pub fn a_thing() {
    println!("This is a module_b thing");
}

pub fn a_second_thing() {
    a_thing();
    println!("This is another module_b thing");
}
```

Then `module_b` will contain two functions named `a_thing` and `a_second_thing`. It's not a problem that those functions have the same names as functions in the `module_a` module from before, because they're in a different module.

 Why did the compiler look in two places for the source code of `module_b`? This allows us to be more flexible in how we lay out our directory structure for our program's source code.

Accessing module contents from outside

In the *A module as a section of a file* section, the `a_second_thing` function is part of the same module as `a_thing`, so it's automatically allowed to use the short version of the other function's name to refer to it. However, code outside of the module needs to use the full name to refer to items inside the module. There are two ways this can be done. It can either be done directly, which is a good choice if we don't expect to be referring to the item often, or we can tell Rust that we want to use the short name for an item in a different module, which is a good choice if we're going to be using that item often in our code.

Using the item's full name directly

An item's full name consists of the module name, a `::` symbol, and then the item's short name. If we have several layers of modules that we need to get through before we find the item we want, we list those modules' names in order, with a `::` between each name. For example, we might refer to `std::path::Path` to get the `Path` item from the `path` module of the `std` module.

We can use the full name anywhere and be completely unambiguous as to what item we're talking about.

Using the item's short name

We can also use the `use` keyword to tell Rust that we want to refer to an item in a different module by its short name. This is done by just writing `use` followed by the full name of the item we want to use. For example, `use std::path::Path;` allows us to use just the short name for that item (`Path` in this example) in the following instructions, until we come to the `}` that closes the section of code where our `use` keyword was written (or we come to the end of the module file, which amounts to the same thing).

We can use the same syntax to tell Rust that we want to use the name of a module, rather than an item in a module. For example, `std::path` is a valid command. That would allow us to use `path::Path` as the name of the `Path` item in subsequent code. This is frequently convenient, since it still keeps the external items boxed up and separate, while providing reasonably short and informative names to work with.

Public and private module items

In many of the preceding examples, we saw a `pub` keyword. That keyword makes the item it's attached to *public*, meaning that it is available to code that is not part of the same module. If we omit the `pub` keyword on an item, that item is `private`, meaning that it can only be accessed within the module where it is defined. Private is the default, so we need to explicitly mark those items that we want to have as part of the module's externally accessible interface as public by using the `pub` keyword.

Making an item private is not a security mechanism. If you're worried that your code will be linked with hostile code that might misuse your code or data, making the code or data private will not protect against such attacks. Rather, the distinction between public and private exists in order to help us make it plain which parts of the code are *intended* for use outside of the current module, and which are meant to be used only internally. This helps us maintain our software, because we are free to make whatever changes we want to to private items, whereas with public items, we have to be careful that our changes do not break external things we might not even be aware exist.

Expressions

The instructions that tell the computer to do something in a Rust program are almost all expressions. An expression tells the computer how to compute a particular value, and produces that value as its result. In math, *2 + 2* is an expression with a resulting value of 4. Similarly, *(2 + 2) - 1* is an expression with a resulting value of 3, which is itself made up of an addition expression and a subtraction expression. In Rust, the same basic idea applies: expressions tell the computer how to find a value, and they can be combined together, because using an expression that produces a value has the same result as using that value directly, just as writing (2 + 2) - 1 has the same result as writing 4 - 1.

Not all expressions in Rust look like math, though. Rust is a programming language, not just a calculator. It's the idea of expressions, which combine values to produce new values, that matters.

Literal expressions

The simplest of Rust's expressions are the ones where we just write out the representation of the value we want. For example, when Rust sees 2 it knows we are asking it for the number 2. Similarly, when Rust sees "Hello, world!" it knows we're asking it to produce the sequence of letters that spells out *Hello, world!*

Rust recognizes the following literal expressions:

- Numbers
- Quoted text
- Byte sequences
- Single Unicode points
- Single bytes
- Boolean values

Numbers can be written as integers or decimal numbers or in engineering notation, and there are a few variants for quoted text and byte sequences, too. Boolean values are written as either true or false. In this book, we're not going to need any of the variants of quoted text, and we won't need byte sequences at all, so we won't go into those in more detail. See https://doc.rust-lang.org/ if you're curious.

Operator expressions

Again, like math, Rust has a number of symbolic **operators** that can be applied to values to transform them into some new value. For example, + is a Rust operator that adds two values together. So, 2 + 2 is a Rust expression adding the number 2 to itself, producing the number 4. Rust also uses – as the subtraction operator, * as the multiplication operator, / as the division operator, and % as the remainder operator.

Rust is not limited to mathematical operators, though. In Rust, & means *and*, | means *or*, ^ means *exclusive or*, ! means *not* (!true is false, for example), << means *leftward bit shift*, and >> means *rightward bit shift*. Sometimes the meanings of those operations depends on the type of value that they're acting on. For example, | means *bitwise or* when applied to integers, but *logical or* when applied to Boolean values.

Then there are the comparison operators. The == operator means *check whether two values are equal*. An expression built around the == operator produces the Boolean value true if the two values being compared are equal, and false if they are not. So, for example, 5 == 4 is an expression producing false as its result. Similarly, != means *not equal*, > means *greater than*, < means *less than*, >= means *greater than or equal*, and <= means *less than or equal*. All of them produce true when the relationship is correct, and false when it is not.

Finally, Rust recognizes && and || operators. These can only be applied to Boolean (true or false) values, and produce the same results as & and | do when applied to the same values. The difference is that && and || are what is called *lazy* or *short-circuit* operators, which means that they will not bother evaluating their right-side operand if the left-side operand provides enough information to determine the operator's produced value. For example, for the expression false && some_expensive_calculation(), Rust will never bother to run the some_expensive_calculation function, because no matter what the function produced as its result, the result of the && operation is going to be false.

In most situations where we'd use & or | on Boolean values, we should use && or || instead, since it allows Rust to be a little more efficient, especially if we're mindful enough to put the more expensive operations on the right side of the operator.

These are not a full list of Rust's operators, and we'll see some of the more specialized ones as we move onward through the language. These are the operators we need for expressing the majority of calculations, computations, and decisions in our programs, though.

Array and tuple expressions

An **array** is a sequential collection of data values. There are many ways to use and manipulate them, but here we're interested in the specialized expressions that create them and access their internal data values. To tell Rust that we want to create a new array, all we have to do is write a [symbol, and then a comma-separated list of expressions that produce the values we want to store in the array, and then a] symbol. There doesn't have to be anything between the beginning and ending symbols if we want an empty array. So, we can write [] as an expression producing an empty array, or [1, 3, 5] as an expression producing an array containing three numbers. All of the values stored in an array need to have the same data type—integers in this case—so trying to set the second element to a text string such as "nope" would produce a compiler error when we tried to compile the program.

That's really nice for cases where we need to create a short array, but imagine writing out an expression for an array containing a thousand values! We wouldn't want to write them out one by one. Fortunately, we can instead do something like [0; 1000], which produces an array containing a thousand zero values. Some other part of our code can then fill in different values in those slots.

Once we have an array value, we often need access to the values stored inside it. That too is achieved using the [and] symbols. If we have an array named an_array (we'll see how to give values names in the *Variables, types, and mutability* section of this chapter), we can access the first value in the array as an_array[0], the second value as an_array[1], and so on. Notice that the first value is numbered with 0, while the second is 1. Many programming languages count this way, because it simplifies some of the math that they frequently need to do with respect to arrays and other sequences of values.

In addition to arrays, Rust allows us to make **tuples**. The expression to create a tuple is similar to that for arrays: (1, "wow", true) is a tuple containing the number value 1, the text value wow, and the Boolean true. If we have a tuple named a_tuple, then a_tuple.1 produces the second value in the tuple, in this case the word wow. There's no simplified way to create a tuple containing a thousand duplicates, though, because that's not what they're for. Unlike arrays, a single tuple can contain values of more than one value type, and they are intended to serve as lightweight data structures, rather than as a collection of many similar data values.

In some languages, the contents of a tuple cannot be changed. That's not how it works in Rust, though, where tuples follow the same rules for that sort of thing as any other data structure.

If we need to make a tuple with only one contained value (which is not common, because the whole point of a tuple is to associate multiple values together), we need to include a comma after the value. So, a single-element tuple containing the number 5 looks like this: `(5,)`

Block expressions

Sometimes, the necessary steps to figure out an expression's result value just don't fit into a single expression of the sorts we've looked at before. Maybe they need to store a data value for a little while in order to execute efficiently, or are otherwise too complex to be reasonably written in the *1 + ((2 * 57) / 13)* style.

That's where block expressions come in. Block expressions look a lot like the body of a function because the body of a function *is* a block expression. They start with { and end with }. Between those two markers, we can write whatever instructions we need, including doing things like defining variables or other named items.

At the very end of the block should come the expression that produces the final result value of the block. So, for example, the block expression `{ 2 + 2; 19 % 3; println!("In a block"); true}` is a (kind of silly) block expression that produces the Boolean `true` as its result, but not until after it has calculated that 2 plus 2 equals 4, and calculated that the remainder of 19 over 3 is 1, and printed out *In a block* to the console.

 By the way, the Rust compiler will warn us about that block expression, because it calculates two values and then just discards them. That's wasteful, so Rust points it out. If optimizations are enabled, the compiler will actually skip generating code to calculate the values at all, but that's an optimization, and the program and compiler are still supposed to act as if they did perform the calculations.

Notice the semicolons (;) in the block expression. Every top-level instruction in the block has a semicolon after it, *except the last one*. That's because the semicolon tells Rust that the expression before it should be treated as a **statement**, which basically means that it won't produce a value, or if it does, we don't care what that value is. In some cases, the semicolon can be left off of expressions prior to the last one in a block, but I don't recommend it, because explicitly discarding the results of expressions whose results we're not going to use allows the compiler more freedom to make inferences and optimizations, and can help avoid some fairly obscure compiler errors.

If we put a ; after the final expression in a block, we're saying that the block doesn't have a meaningful resulting value at all. In that case, it ends up having () as its resulting value. That's an empty tuple, which is a pretty good way of saying: *Nothing to see here, folks*. () is used that way throughout the Rust language and libraries.

Branch expressions

One of the things that makes programs truly useful is the ability for them to make decisions. We can do that in Rust by using an if expression. An if expression looks something like this:

```
if 3 > 4 {
    println!("Uh-oh. Three is greater than four.");
}
else if 3 == 4 {
    println!("There seems to be something wrong with math.");
}
else {
    println!("Three is not greater than or equal to four.");
};
```

If you're familiar with other programming languages, you might be wondering where the parenthesis are around the condition expression. Rust's syntax doesn't call for parenthesis there. In fact, if we place the condition in parenthesis, the compiler will warn us that they're not necessary.

What we have here is an expression that shows off all the features of an if. It starts off with the keyword if, followed by a *condition expression* that produces either true or false, and then a block expression. If the condition expression produces true, the block expression is run, but if the condition expression produces false, the block expression is not run.

Using 3 > 4 as our condition expression is not very useful. We might as well just write false, or leave that block expression out entirely since it will never run. However, in real code, we would use a condition expression whose result we would not know at the time we were writing the code. *Is it between the hours of 8 A.M. and 5 P.M., Did the user select this value from the menu,* and *Does the value match what is stored in the database* are examples of more realistic conditions, though of course they would have to be expressed in Rust.

After that, we have an `else if` and another condition expression and block. That means that, if the first condition expression produced `false`, the computer should check whether the second one produces `true`, and if it does, run the associated block expression.

We can chain as many `else if` expressions as we want after an initial `if`, so there's no limit to the number of different options we can make available to the computer. However, only one of them will run after any given decision. The computer will start with the initial `if` and check the values of the conditional expressions one at a time until it finds one that produces `true`, then it will run the associated block expression, and then it will be done with the if expression and move on to the subsequent instructions.

After an `if` and any `else if` we might wish to include, we are allowed to put an `else` followed by a block expression. This is a branch without a condition, and what it means is *if none of the condition expressions produced* `true`, *do this*. In other words, it allows us to tell the computer what to do by default, if none of the special cases we provided apply.

Loop expressions

Another of the basic abilities that make programs useful is looping. Rust has several different kinds of loops, but we're going to look at two of them here: `while` loops and `for` loops.

while loops

A `while` loop is a lot like an `if` expression. The difference is, instead of checking the condition expression once and then either running the block expression or not, and then being done, a `while` loop keeps repeating the process until the condition expression produces `false`. So, if the condition expression results in `false` right away, the block expression never runs. On the other hand, if the condition expression produces `true` on the first check, the block expression gets run, and then the condition expression is evaluated again. If it produces `true` again, the block runs again, and so on, until the condition expression finally produces `false`.

That means that it's very important for the block expression to change something that affects the condition expression's result. If the condition expression produces `true` and the block doesn't have any chance of changing that, the program will be stuck looping through that block over and over until the program is forcefully terminated. This is the easiest way to cause your program to freeze.

So, here's a simple `while` loop:

```
while i < 3 {
    i = i + 1;
    println!("While loop {}", i);
}
```

We're using a variable named `i` here, which we'll talk about more in the *Variables and mutability* section of this chapter. For now, just think of `i` as a name that we can assign different values to at different times, sort of like how we can ask different people to sit in the same chair at different times.

So, we have the `while` keyword followed by a condition expression. This condition expression uses a variable, which we change the value of in the block expression, so we're not in danger of looping forever. If `i` starts with the value 0, we should see the block expression run three times: once when `i` is 0, once when `i` is 1, and once when `i` is 2. When `i` gets to 3, the condition expression produces `false` as its result (3 is not less than 3), and the loop stops.

for loops

Sometimes, `while` loops are exactly what we need, but the two most common needs for looping are to loop a specific number of times or to use a loop to process each element contained in an array or similar data structure. In both of these cases, `for` loops work better.

A `for` loop runs its block expression once for each value produced by an **iterator**. An iterator is a special kind of data value that has the job of returning a sequence of values, one at a time. An iterator for an array, for example, produces a different member of the array each time we ask it for a value.

To loop a specific number of times, we can use a `for` loop along with a **range expression**, which is an expression that produces an iterator over a sequence of numbers. Let's look at a concrete example of that:

```
for num in 3..7 {
    println!("for loop {}", num);
}
```

We started off with the `for` keyword and then `num`, which is the name which is going to be given to each value that the iterator produces, one at a time, as those values are processed by the `for` loop. Then comes another keyword, `in`. Finally, the expression that produces our iterator. In this case, we have a range expression, which represents the values 3, 4, 5, and 6. Notice that 7 is not included in the range. As with counting from zero, this makes some of the math easier for the computer to do, and in this case, it makes things easier for us most of the time as well. If we want to loop seven times, we could just write `0..7`.

There is a variant we could use that would include the final number in the output, should we need it: `3..=7`. Just remember that if you loop through `0..=7`, you're going to be running the block expression eight times.

The other time when `for` loops shine is when we have a collection of actual values that we want to process, as the following example:

```
for word in ["Hello", "world", "of", "loops"].iter() {
    println!("{}", word);
}
```

This loop prints out each of the words in the array, each on their own line. The `word` name is set to the first value produced by the iterator, `"Hello"`, and the block expression is run. Then `word` is set to the second value produced by the iterator, `"world"`, and the block expression is run again. This continues until the iterator runs out of values to produce, and then stops.

Here, our iterator is producing the values stored in an array. The `.iter()` part of that expression is saying, basically: *Arrays know how to make iterators for themselves, so ask the array to give us an iterator.* We'll see more about how to implement functions that are specific to a data type in a later chapter, but for now, we just need to know that that's what the `.` symbol means: the thing on the right of the dot is specific to the thing on the left. We are asking the computer to run, not just any `iter` function, but the `iter` function that is associated with our array.

Variables, types, and mutability

A variable is a named box in which a data value can be stored. The variable itself isn't the data value, just like a carton of milk is not the same thing as milk (it's waxed cardboard and such *containing* milk).

On the other hand, if somebody needs milk and you hand them a full milk carton, they're not going to complain, and the same goes for Rust. If a Rust expression needs an integer, and we provide a variable containing an integer, Rust will be perfectly happy with that.

Variables are most often created using the `let` keyword:

```
let x = 10;
```

This statement creates a variable called x containing the 10 value in it. Once that's done, we can refer to x as part of the expressions. For example, x + 5 is now a valid expression, with a resulting value of 15.

> The names that `for` loops use are also variables, as are function parameters, although they are not created with the `let` keyword.

In addition to having a name, variables are characterized by the type of value they can store. Each variable can store one kind of value, and can never store any other type of information. Rust can often figure out what type of information a given variable can store, but we always have the option of being explicit about it. If we tell Rust that `let x: i32 = 99;` then Rust will make sure that the x variable can store a 32-bit signed integer and report an error if we try to store something else there. On the other hand, `let x: f64 = 999.0;` tells Rust that we want x to store a 64-bit floating-point number and that trying to store anything else there is an error.

We don't have to provide an initial value for a variable. For example, we could say `let x: u16;` to tell Rust that the x variable needs to be able to store 16-bit unsigned integers. That's fine. However, if it's even possible that some of our code will try to use the contents of the variable without first having stored some contents there to be used, the Rust compiler will consider that an error. It's usually easier to just provide a starting value when we create a variable.

Variables are called **variables** because the values they contain can be changed. Except in Rust, by default, they can't. Rust allows us to use multiple `let` statements to create new variables with the same names as old variables, but we can't just assign a new value to an existing variable, unless that variable is **mutable**.

Creating a new variable with the same name as an existing variable is called **shadowing** the old variable. A shadowed variable still contains the value it did before, but cannot be accessed by name any more, because that name now belongs to a different variable. If there are any references to the old variable still in play, they will still be accessing the old variable, though, not the new one.

Being mutable just means that the variable will accept changes, up to and including a whole new value. We use the `mut` keyword to tell Rust that a variable should be mutable:

```
let mut x = 17;
```

The new x variable is mutable. That means we can modify its contents:

```
x = 0;
```

Instead of containing 17, x now contains 0.

The equal symbol (=) that we're using for variables is not a statement of mathematical equality. It doesn't mean: *These two things are defined as being the same.* Instead it means: *Right here, right now, the value produced by the expression on the right side of the = is to be stored in the variable on the left.* This would be nonsense in math, but it makes perfect sense in Rust:

```
for i in 0..5 {
    x = x + i;
}
```

Rust has quite a lot of built-in data types. We've seen `i32`, `f64`, and `u16`, which are 32-bit signed integer, 64-bit floating point, and 16-bit unsigned integer, respectively. There are also more types following the same pattern, such as `u64` for an unsigned 64-bit integer, as well as types such as `bool` for Boolean values; `isize` and `usize` for signed and unsigned integers that take up the same number of bits as a memory address on the target architecture; and `char` and `str` for single Unicode code points and sequences of them.

These are known as primitive types, because they're inherent to the language. However, Rust also allows us to create new types, and so the Rust standard library contains many more data types that are suited to various specific uses, and there are even more available in third-party libraries.

Type inference

As we noticed earlier, we can specify the type of a variable, but we often don't have to. That's because Rust has a feature called type inference, which often lets it figure out what type a variable is by looking at what we do with it. For example, if we were using the Tokio networking library, we might use code such as this:

```
let addr = "127.0.0.1:12345".parse()?;
let tcp = TcpListener::bind(&addr)?;
```

We didn't specify what type the `addr` variable should have. Even more interesting, we didn't tell the text address what kind of information we needed it to parse into.

 Parsing means *transforming a representation into usable data*, approximately. Lots of things can be represented as a string of text, if you know how to parse that text into the information you really want.

 The question marks in this example are part of Rust's error handling mechanism, and the ampersand is an operator that affects how the `addr` variable is shared with the function. We'll see more on both of those soon.

However, Rust can see that we're passing the `addr` variable (or rather, a reference to it, but more on that in the next chapter) as a parameter of the `TcpListener::bind` function, and it knows that that function needs a reference to a `SocketAddr`, so `addr` must be a `SocketAddr`. Then, since it has figured out that `addr` is a `SocketAddr`, it takes it a step further and determines that it should use the string parsing function that produces a `SocketAddr` as its resulting value.

Type inference can save an amazing amount of time in a language as strict as Rust. On the other hand, it can be surprising if you see an error message about a data type you've never heard of, because Rust decided that it was the one you needed. If that happens, try assigning the type you actually expect to your variable and see what the Rust compiler has to say afterward.

Data structures

Creating a data structure is one of the ways to add a new data type to Rust. A data structure is a group of variables that have been attached to each other, resulting in a single new data type that means *all of these, together*.

A new structure is defined using the `struct` keyword:

```
pub struct Constrained {
    pub min: i32,
    pub max: i32,
    current: i32,
}
```

 Notice the commas after each contained variable is defined. It can be tempting to use semicolons there, but that would cause a compiler error. The final comma is optional, but recommended, because it means that the lines can be rearranged without having to pay attention to where a comma might be missing, among other reasons.

Here, we've defined a structure called `Constrained`, which is made up of three different 32-bit unsigned integer variables. The structure itself is public, meaning that it can be used outside of the module where it's defined.

The `min` and `max` contained variables are also public, but that means something slightly different. It means that anywhere we have a `Constrained` value, we can access the `min` and `max` contained values directly. The `current` value, on the other hand, is private, which means that it can be directly accessed only within the module where the structure is defined. We can define functions in that module with the express purpose of accessing the data contained in private structure members, but the members themselves are not part of the structure's public interface, even if the structure itself is public.

To access `min` and `max`, we can use the same `.` symbol that we've seen previously in a few places. So, if `cons` is a mutable `Constrained` value, then we can do things like this:

```
cons.min = 5;
```

Mutability of data structures

We cannot use the `mut` keyword to make the contained values within a structure mutable, and leaving the keyword off does not make them immutable. Instead, the entire structure is mutable or immutable on a case-by-case basis. See the following, for example:

```
let change_no: Constrained;
let mut change_yes: Constrained;
```

The preceding code means that there are two variables, both with `Constrained` as their data type, but the value stored in `change_no` is immutable while the value stored in `change_yes` is mutable.

More about functions

Now, we're going to fill in the blanks left in the earlier discussion of functions by talking about parameters and return types.

Parameters

Parameters allow us to provide information to a function at the time when we ask it to run.

 Asking a function to run is called *calling* it.

When we define a function, we can tell it the variable names and types we want it to use for receiving parameters, as in the following example:

```
pub fn set(&mut self, value: i32) {
    self.current = value;
}
```

We'll talk about `self` in the *Implementing behavior for types* section of this chapter. For now, ignore it and take a look at `value`. Here, we've provided a name and data type, just as we would if we were using `let` to create a new variable. What we have not done is provide a value for the `value` variable, because that happens when the function is called.

We've seen function calls all along, but for the sake of clarity, they look like this:

```
some_function(2 + 2, false)
```

In that example, `some_function` is the name of a function, and the values that are assigned to its parameters are the results of the expressions `2 + 2` and `false`. The parameter expressions are evaluated *before* the function is called, so the actual values of the parameters are the number `4` and the Boolean, `false`.

Return types

Calling a function is an expression, which means it produces a resulting value. We've been ignoring that until now. If a function is going to produce a resulting value, we have to tell the compiler what data type that result will have. We do that like this:

```
pub fn get(&self) -> i32 {
    if self.current < self.min {
        return self.min;
    }
    else if self.current > self.max {
        return self.max;
    }
    else {
        return self.current;
    };
}
```

That's a longish example, but for now we're focusing on the first line. After the function parameters, we see `->    i32`. That tells Rust that the `get` function has `i32` as the data type of its result. Once it knows that, the compiler will make sure that it's true. In this example, there's no path through the function that doesn't produce an `i32` value, so the compiler is happy with it.

We also used the `return` keyword in that example. A `return` statement stops the currently running function (meaning that any instructions that would have run after the `return` statement do not in fact get run) and provides the resulting value for the function call expression. In this example, if the current value is less than the minimum value, the minimum value is returned. If the current value is greater than the maximum value, the maximum value is returned. Otherwise, the current value is returned.

You may recall that in Rust, function bodies are block expressions, and `if` along with its riders is also an expression, which means they all produce a resulting value naturally, even when we don't use the `return` keyword. That means that we could have written the example function this way and gotten the same result:

```
pub fn alternate_get(&self) -> i32 {
    if self.current < self.min {
```

```
        self.min
    }
    else if self.current > self.max {
        self.max
    }
    else {
        self.current
    }
}
```

Do you see the difference? Before, we used `return` to specifically terminate the function and provide a resulting value. Here, the resulting value of the function's block expression is the resulting value of the `if` expression, which is the resulting value of the block expression for whichever branch it follows, which is either `self.min`, `self.max` or `self.current`. The end result is the same, but it's expressed differently.

Error handling

Sometimes, we can anticipate the possibility that something could go wrong, or we're using a library function that knows it might not succeed. When that happens, we'll find ourselves using the special `Result` data type. The result is a **generic type**, which we'll talk about in a later chapter, but it's so integral to using functions that we're going to see how to use it here in a rote way.

A function that can fail will have a return type something like this:
`Result<i32, &'static str>`. This looks kind of nuts at first glance, I admit. Let's break it down. The type starts off with `Result` followed by a <, then `i32`, then a , , then `&'static str`, and finally a >. What that means is that the function will produce an `i32` if it succeeds, and an `&'static str` if it fails. `&'static str` happens to be the type for a literal text expression, like `oops, it broke,` so what we're really saying here is that the function will return an integer or an error message.

 It's common to have a data type specifically for representing errors, such as an `Error` structure, rather than just using a textual error message.

Using Result to signal success or failure

Expanding on our example, how do we write a function that can either succeed or fail? See the following:

```
fn can_fail(x: bool) -> Result<i32, &'static str> {
    if x {
        return Ok(5);
    }
    else {
        return Err("x is false");
    };
}
```

First, we set up the return type to use Result, then, in the body of the function, we use either Ok() or Err() to signal that we're returning a valid value or an error, respectively.

If a function might fail, but doesn't have any meaningful return value if it succeeds, we can use () as the successful return type. So, in that case the return type might look like this: Result<(), &'static str>. The successful return value would be Ok(()).

Calling functions that return Result

When we call a function that returns Result, the return value is—as requested—a Result, rather than the data type we really need. There are several ways of working with that, depending on our specific needs.

The simplest way to deal with a Result is to use the ? operator, which extracts the stored value from a successful Result, or returns a Result containing the error value if the Result it's looking at indicates an error. Because ? might return from the current function in the same way that a return statement would, ? can only be used in functions that themselves return Result and use the same data type to represent errors. Using ? looks like this:

```
let mut cons: Constrained = new_constrained(0, 10, 5)?;
```

Here, we're calling the new_constrained function, which returns either a successful result or an error message. However, the variable we're assigning to has Constrained as its type, not Result. That works because of the ? at the end, which pulls out the Constrained value if the function call succeeds, and returns if the function call fails.

The next easiest way to deal with a returned `Result` is to use the `expect` function. This function does something similar to the `?`, pulling out the success value if Result indicates success, but it handles failure differently. Instead of returning an error from the current function, `expect` terminates the whole program and prints out an error message. Functions that use `expect` don't have to return a `Result`, so it can be used in some situations where `?` is unavailable. Using `expect` looks like this:

```
let mut cons: Constrained = new_constrained(0, 10, 5).expect("Something
went very wrong");
```

The parameter passed to `expect` is the error message it should display on failure. There are some other functions, similar to `expect`, that handle errors in various ways, such as calling an error handler function.

Finally, we can actually handle the errors ourselves, by checking whether the returned `Result` is an `Ok` or an `Err`. That is done by using the `match` or `if let` expressions, which we will learn about in `Chapter 4`, the *Making Decisions by Pattern Matching*.

Implementing behavior for types

In previous examples, we've seen what appeared to be calls to functions that were contained within data values, such as `"127.0.0.1:12345".parse()` or `["Hello", "world", "of", "loops"].iter()`. Those are functions that have been **implemented** on the type of those values. Implementing functions on a type looks like this:

```
impl Constrained {
    pub fn set(&mut self, value: i32) {
        self.current = value;
    }

    pub fn get(&self) -> i32 {
        if self.current < self.min {
            return self.min;
        }
        else if self.current > self.max {
            return self.max;
        }
        else {
            return self.current;
        };
    }
}
```

This is an implementation block (which is *not* a block expression) for a data type, in this case the `Constrained` type that we created earlier. Implementation blocks are introduced with the `impl` keyword, then they have the name of the type that we want to place our functions *inside of*, and then the functions we want to add to the data type, between the { and } symbols.

 While we can access functions that were implemented on a type as if they were variables contained in data values of that type, they're not actually stored within the memory holding the data value. There's no need for each data value to have copies of the functions, since the copies would all be identical anyway.

Functions implemented on a type can be public or private, depending on whether we want them to be used by external users of the data type, or only by other functions within the current module.

When a function is implemented on a type, the first parameter is special. It's automatically provided to the function, even though it is not passed as a function parameter when we call the function. This automatic parameter is traditionally called `self`. It is the job of `self` to give the function access to the data value that it is being called through, meaning that if we do something like `"127.0.0.1".parse()`, the parse function receives `"127.0.0.1"` as its `self` parameter. The `self` parameter can be written as `self`, `&self`, or `&mut self`, a choice that we'll discuss in the next chapter.

The syntax of an implementation block allows us to specify which data type we're implementing functions on. Could we implement functions on types we didn't create, such as `i32` or `SocketAddr`? The answer is yes, but only if we create a *trait*. We'll see more about traits in `Chapter 5`, *One data Type Representing Multiple Kinds of Data*. Without using traits, we're only able to implement functions on data types we created within the same project, although they do not have to be in the same module.

Summary

As we put the things we've learned in this chapter into practice, our grasp on them will solidify. We've learned about the basic structure of Rust programs, as well as how to write functions, loops, and branches. In addition, we've learned about Rust's type system and how to attach behavior to a data type. These things give us a foundation to build on, while we learn about the things that make Rust truly different from other programming languages.

In the next chapter, we're going to look at how the fundamental Rust concepts of ownership and borrowing work.

3
The Big Ideas – Ownership and Borrowing

Ownership and borrowing are the features that set Rust apart from other programming languages. The closest equivalent that you're likely to find is the **Resource Aquisition Is Instantiation (RAII)** design pattern common in C++, but that's a design pattern, not a language feature, and is not fully analogous.

In this chapter, we're going to talk about the following:

- Ownership of values and the scope of variables
- The ways that ownership is transferred between scopes
- Borrowing and lending data values, and how that interacts with ownership
- The lifetime of borrowed values
- The `self` parameter of functions, and the implications of borrowing or not borrowing it

Scope and ownership

In Rust, every data value has a single owning scope—no more, no less. So, what's a scope? The easy answer is that a scope is the place where a block expression stores its variables. Scopes are not directly represented in the source code, but a scope begins when a block expression begins, with a { symbol, and ends when the block expression ends, with } (or when a `return` statement is run before the block reaches its end). The scope is the chunk of memory where the block's variables are stored.

Every data value has an owning scope, including implied temporary values such as the result of 2 + 2 when we ask Rust to compute (2 + 2) * 3.

When Rust is done with a scope, all of the data values that scope owns are discarded and the memory that was used to store them is freed up for other uses. This includes memory that was allocated on the **heap**, which we'll learn how to use in Chapter 6, *Heap Memory and Smart Pointers*.

The time between when a value is created and the time when its owning scope is done is called the **lifetime** of the value.

The stack

Like most programming languages, Rust uses a **stack** to handle memory management for scopes. A stack is a simple data structure, also referred to as a **Last In, First Out Queue** or **LIFO**. Stacks support two operations: **push**, which stores a new value, and pop, which removes and returns the most recently stored value.

We can think of a stack as a pile of boxes. If we want to remove the stuff stored in the top box, we can just take it down and look inside. However, if we want to remove the stuff stored in one of the boxes underneath, we first have to remove the boxes above it. Here's a diagram of what I'm talking about, with access to the boxes underneath blocked by the ones above them:

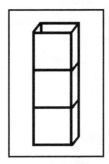

When a Rust block expression starts, it makes a note of how tall the stack is and, when the block ends, it removes things from the stack until the stack is the same height as it was to begin with. In between, when the block needs to store a new value, it pushes that value onto the stack.

When a value is removed from the stack, the Rust compiler also makes sure to do any cleanup that is needed before discarding the value, including calling a custom cleanup function for the value if one is defined.

Most programming languages do this, but not exclusively. In Rust, even when a data value uses heap memory, it is represented on the stack and controlled by the rules of ownership. By following that simple procedure, it's easy for Rust to handle all of the record keeping and memory management for a program, efficiently and with no garbage collection required.

Garbage collection is a mechanism used in many programming languages to remove the burden of memory management from the programmer. It's even easier to use than Rust's method, but it does require time for the garbage collection mechanism to run, which can impact program performance. Rust's method is almost entirely deterministic at compile time: the Rust compiler knows when to allocate and deallocate memory without having to figure it out while the program runs.

Transferring ownership

It's possible (and common) to transfer ownership of a value to a different scope. For example, we can do something like this:

```
{
    let main_1 = Point2D {x: 10.0, y: 10.0};
    receive_ownership(main_1);
    receive_ownership(main_1); // This will cause a compiler error!
}
```

What is happening is that the `main_1` variable is created and initialized under the ownership of the current scope (the value is pushed onto the stack), but then the ownership is transferred to the scope of the block expression that makes up the `receive_ownership` function's body, when the value is used as a function parameter. The compiler knows that the current scope is no longer responsible for cleaning up the value stored in `main_1`, because that job now belongs to a different scope.

The bytes that represent the value on the stack are copied to a new location on the stack, within the scope that is receiving ownership. Most data values store some of their information outside of the stack, though, so the bytes that are left behind in the old scope are considered no longer meaningful or safe to use.

If we try to use the value stored in `main_1` after it has been moved to a different scope, as we're doing here with the second call to `receive_ownership`, the compiler will report an error. It's not just using the value as a function parameter that will cause an error, either. Any use of a value that has been moved is an error. It's no longer there to be used.

Ownership can also be transferred in the other direction. This function receives ownership of its parameter, but then returns the parameter (and hence the ownership) back to the block where it was called:

```
pub fn receive_ownership(point: Point2D) -> Point2D {
    println!("Point2D{{x: {}, y: {}}} is now owned by a new scope",
point.x, point.y);
    return point;
}
```

That doesn't mean that the original variable (`main_1`) becomes usable again, but if we assign the return value from the function to a variable, we can continue using that value through the new variable.

Ownership can also be transferred "sideways" by assigning a value to a different variable. We do something like this:

```
let mut main_4 = main_2;
```

Here, the value stored in `main_2` is moved to `main_4`. In this basic example, that's not particularly interesting; we've just got a new variable containing the value that the old variable used to contain, and they're both in the same scope anyway. This gets more interesting when we do things like assigning a value to a structure member, especially when the structure has a different lifetime.

Rust's compiler is very careful about ownership, and when it detects a situation where ownership is not properly respected, or even *might not* be properly respected, it reports an error. The following function will not compile, because it is only valid when the `switch` parameter is `false`:

```
pub fn uncertain_ownership(switch: bool) {
    let point = Point2D {x: 3.0, y: 3.0};

    if switch {
        receive_ownership(point);
    }

    println!("point is Point2D{{x: {}, y: {}}}", point.x, point.y);
}
```

When we try to compile the `uncertain_ownership` function, we get output like this from the compiler:

```
error[E0382]: use of moved value: `point.x`
  --> src/main.rs:18:50
   |
15 |          receive_ownership(point);
   |                            ----- value moved here
...
18 |      println!("point is Point2D{{x: {}, y: {}}}", point.x, point.y);
   |                                                   ^^^^^^^ value used here after move
   |
   = note: move occurs because `point` has type `Point2D`, which does not implement the `Copy` trait
error[E0382]: use of moved value: `point.y`
  --> src/main.rs:18:59
   |
15 |          receive_ownership(point);
   |                            ----- value moved here
...
18 |      println!("point is Point2D{{x: {}, y: {}}}", point.x, point.y);
   |                                                            ^^^^^^^ value used here after move
   |
   = note: move occurs because `point` has type `Point2D`, which does not implement the `Copy` trait
```

As far as the compiler is concerned, if we could have moved the value before using it, we don't get to use it.

Copying

In the compiler error discussed at the end of the *Transferring ownership* section of this chapter, we see that the compiler noted that the data value is moved because it *does not implement the* `Copy` *trait*, which is interesting. What does that mean?

For some data types, particularly the primitive types such as integers and floating-point numbers, copying the bytes that represent them on the stack is all that is required to actually make a complete working copy of the data value. In other words, their representation does not refer to anything stored elsewhere in memory or otherwise rely on ownership to keep everything correct.

There are a number of data types in the standard library that could have the `Copy` trait as far as memory usage is concerned, but make use of ownership to keep other things safe and correct. Examples include data types that represent access to external resources such as files or network sockets, and data types having to do with concurrency. Ownership has turned out to be an even more powerful tool than was originally expected.

Data types that do not rely on ownership at all are said to have the `Copy` trait. We'll see how to declare that our own data types have the Copy trait in Chapter 8, *Important Standard Traits*.

When a value's data type has the Copy trait, Rust doesn't move the value when it is transferred. The receiver still receives the value, but the old value remains valid. Instead of moving, the value has been copied. This function has almost exactly the same structure as the `uncertain_ownership` function, which refuses to compile:

```
pub fn copied_ownership(switch: bool) {
    let local = 4.0;

    if switch {
        receive_ownership(Point2D {x: local, y: 4.0});
    }

    println!("x is {}", x);
}
```

The important difference here is that `local` contains a floating-point value and the floating-point data types have the Copy trait, which means that even though the value of `local` is placed inside of a `Point2D` structure, and that structure is then moved to the `receive_ownership` function's scope, `local` remains valid in the current scope. That's because the value of `local` wasn't moved into `Point2D`. It was copied.

The fact that we used a structure initializer to assign the value of `local` instead of using an = symbol makes no difference. Either way, it's an assignment, and either way, the data type's Copy trait determines whether the assignment is a copy or a move.

Lending

There's one more way we can send information to a different scope and that is by **lending**. When we move a data value, the receiving scope becomes the value's new owner. When we copy a data value, the receiving scope owns the duplicate it received, and the sending scope retains ownership of the original. When we lend a data value, things can get more complicated, because the original scope retains ownership, but the receiving scope is still allowed to access the data.

The original scope still owns the data, which means that, when that scope ends, the data will go away. If some of the scope's contained data was still loaned to a different scope at that time, the program would likely crash and, since the Rust compiler hates potential crashes, it does not allow us to get into that situation. Instead, it requires that any borrowed information must be returned before the owning scope's time is up.

When a data value is borrowed, that value is neither copied nor moved. The bytes that represent that value on the stack stay right where they were. Instead, the borrower receives the memory address of those bytes on the stack, allowing it to violate the conceptual idea of a stack by accessing information stored below the top, probably in a different scope entirely. You can see why the compiler wants to be careful about that!

A currently borrowed data value can't be changed by the owner, even if the data value is stored in a mutable variable. This is part of keeping lending from causing problems: a data value can only ever be changed in one place at a time at most and, when it *can* be changed, it's never in use elsewhere.

Lending immutably

When lending, the default is to lend the data **immutably**, meaning that the borrowed data can be read, but not changed. We can lend immutably to more than one borrower at the same time, which is safe because none of them can change the borrowed data, and so they can't interfere with each other by changing the data value unexpectedly.

To create an immutable borrow, we prefix the expression producing the data value with &, like this:

```
borrow_ownership(&main_3);
```

Here, we're calling a function called `borrow_ownership`, and passing it a data value borrowed from the `main_3` variable.

Lending mutably

Sometimes, we want to lend a data value and allow the receiver to modify it, so that, after the borrow has ended, the data value in the owning scope has changed. When that's what we need, we lend the data **mutably**.

We can't lend mutably unless the data value we're lending is stored in a mutable variable, which means that the mut keyword was used when we declared the variable, like so:

```
let mut main_4 = main_2;
```

Given that we have a mutable variable to lend, we can create a mutable borrow of that variable's value, by using the mut keyword *again*, in a different context:

```
borrow_ownership_mutably(&mut main_4);
```

If there's a mutable borrow of a data value, creating another borrow for it (of either sort) is impossible and, if there are any immutable borrows, then creating a mutable borrow is impossible. That rule means that if a data value is mutably borrowed, it's not borrowed anywhere else. Combined with the rule we discussed earlier that prevents borrowed data from being changed by its real owner, that means that as long as there's a mutable borrow active, that borrow is the only way to modify the borrowed data value.

However, once the borrow is finished, the owner regains control of the (possibly modified) data value.

Accessing borrowed data

To receive borrowed data, we need to properly specify the data type as a borrow. That is done by using & or &mut with the data type on the receiving end, just as we used them with the data value on the sending end.

While the term *borrow* is common in Rust, the technical term is **reference**. So, we will usually say we are borrowing data, using borrowed data, or that a data value is accessed as a borrow, but we could also say that we are referencing data, using referenced data, or that a data value is accessed by reference.

Here, we have the definition of two functions, the same two functions we used in our previous examples. Look at the data types specified for the `point` parameter on each one:

```
pub fn borrow_ownership(point: &Point2D) {
    println!("Point2D{{x: {}, y: {}}} is now borrowed by a new scope",
point.x, point.y);
}

pub fn borrow_ownership_mutably(point: &mut Point2D) {
    println!("Point2D{{x: {}, y: {}}} is now borrowed by a new scope",
point.x, point.y);
    point.x = 13.5;
    println!("Borrowed value changed to Point2D{{x: {}, y: {}}}", point.x,
point.y);
}
```

Being a borrow or mutable borrow is part of the data type for the parameter. That means that the compiler knows the value passed to the parameter must be a borrow and will refuse to compile code that tries to pass a non-borrowed value to the function.

Most of the time, using a borrowed value is the same as using a non-borrowed value, as we can see in these functions. They interact with `point` just as if it were a locally owned variable.

However, that's because the compiler is smart. The truth is that a borrow is a memory address for a data value, not the data value itself (which is the bytes stored in memory *at* that address). Most of the time, the compiler can figure out that it needs to take the extra step of looking in the local variable for the address, then looking in memory at that address for the data, rather than just looking in the local variable for the data.

 This process is called **dereferencing**. For some reason, nobody ever says **deborrowing**.

There are times when the compiler can't figure out that we want to dereference and handle it automatically. In those situations, we can use the * symbol to manually dereference a borrowed value.

The most common place where this comes up is in assigning to a borrowed value. If the borrowed value is a structure or something that has internal data, we can assign to the internal data with no problem, but when we want to assign a whole new value to a borrowed variable, we need to use dereferencing.

This code tries to assign the value as if it weren't a borrow:

```
pub fn set_to_six(value: &mut u32) {
    value = 6;
}
```

We see that `value` is a mutable borrow of a 32-bit unsigned integer. When we try to assign to that variable directly, the compiler tells us this:

```
error[E0308]: mismatched types
  --> src/main.rs:42:13
   |
42 |         value = 6;
   |                 ^
   |
   |                 |
   |                 expected &mut u32, found integral variable
   |                 help: consider mutably borrowing here: `&mut 6`
   |
   = note: expected type `&mut u32`
              found type `{integer}`
```

What's happening here is that there's no way for the compiler to tell the difference between *I want to assign this value to be what is stored in memory at the referenced location* and *I want this reference variable to refer to a different memory location*. It needs to assume one of those and let us tell it if we want the other, and the assumption it picks is the second one.

 It makes sense to pick *assign a new value to this variable* as the default, since that's what = means in any other situation as well. Working with borrowed data is a special case, not the default.

The advice given by the compiler here is also based on the assumption that what we want to do is have `value` refer to a new memory address, which means that if we were to follow it blindly, the compiler error would go away, but the program would not do what we want. Instead of storing the number 6 in the borrowed variable, it would set the `value` variable to contain a new borrow.

What we actually want to do is this:

```
pub fn set_to_six(value: &mut u32) {
    *value = 6;
}
```

That tells the compiler that instead of assigning *to* value, we want to assign *through* value to the originally borrowed variable.

The ∗ symbol can be used for both reading and writing the borrowed value, and can be used even when not strictly required if we want to be explicit.

Even though dereferencing and multiplication are written using the same symbol, the compiler never gets them confused. Multiplication is not a valid operation on a borrow, and dereferencing isn't a valid operation on a number. Additionally, multiplication always needs a data value on both sides of the ∗, while dereferencing always needs a data value on only one side. Between those two pieces of information, the compiler has more than enough to know which operation we're asking for.

The lifetime of borrowed data

Borrows can not last longer than the data value that they're borrowing. The Rust compiler has to make sure that no part of the program could allow that to happen, which means that it has to keep track of the **lifetime** of every borrow. In the examples we've seen so far, that's easy, because each borrow was created when we called a function and ended when the function returned, while the values that were borrowed lived until the end of the block expression that contained the function calls.

The lifetimes of the borrows were obviously shorter than the lifetimes of the variables, beginning later and ending sooner.

However, it's not hard to create situations where the compiler needs us to give it a hint about how long a borrow can exist, or how long the borrowed value will remain valid. We've already seen that once, when we used `&'static str` as the error type in `Result`. As we now know, this is an immutable reference to `str`, but there's still that `'static` part to understand.

When we write something such as `'static` or `'a` after an `&` symbol, we're telling Rust that the lifetime of that reference has a name, which it recognizes because all lifetime names start with the `'` symbol. If we say that a borrow's lifetime is named `'a`, then we can use that name elsewhere to describe the relationship of that lifetime with the lifetimes of other borrows.

The static lifetime is special, because it's used for data values that are always available, as long as the program is running, such as the string constants we used as error messages in our examples earlier.

It's most useful to give names to lifetimes when we're defining functions, because we don't know what data values are going to be filled in to the function's parameter variables. If some of those parameters are borrows, we need to be able to tell Rust what our expectations are about the lifetimes of those borrows, so it can make sure that the code that calls our functions is doing it correctly.

Here is a function that Rust can't safely compile, because it needs to know more about the lifetimes than we've told it (yet):

```
pub fn smaller_x(value1: &Point2D, value2: &Point2D) -> &f64 {
    if value1.x < value2.x {
        &value1.x
    }
    else {
        &value2.x
    }
}
```

The problem here is that we're receiving two borrowed parameters in this function, each of which could have a different lifetime, and returning another borrowed value . Unfortunately, the Rust compiler doesn't know which parameter the return value will be borrowed from or what its lifetime is, and so it can't properly check the use of that value with code that calls our smaller_x function. Since it can't be sure everything is correct, the compiler simply refuses to try.

We can fix this by adding lifetime annotations:

```
pub fn smaller_x<'a>(value1: &'a Point2D, value2: &'a Point2D) -> &'a f64 {
    if value1.x < value2.x {
        &value1.x
    }
    else {
        &value2.x
    }
}
```

What we've done here is use the name 'a for the lifetimes of all three borrowed values, and also put 'a between < and >, between the function name and the parameter list. The < and > mark the beginning and end of the function's **generic parameter** list, which we'll talk about more in Chapter 7, *Generic Types*. For now, what's important is that we're telling Rust that there is a lifetime that is equal to *or shorter than* the actual lifetimes of both value1 and value2, which is called 'a, and that the return value is safe to use within that 'a lifetime.

Specifying a lifetime name *never* changes the actual lifetime of a borrow. If value1 and value2 have different lifetimes, specifying 'a for them here doesn't make one of them last longer, nor does it shorten the span of the other one. When applied to the parameters, a lifetime name tells Rust that the named lifetime must be *compatible with* that parameter, meaning that the named lifetime must be wholly contained within the actual lifetime of the parameter. Then, when we use the same name for the return value's lifetime, we're telling Rust that the return value will only be guaranteed to be valid within the same limits—in this case, while *both* of the parameters are still valid.

Rust uses that guarantee to check the calling code. If we tried something like this, the Rust compiler would refuse, because we're trying to use the returned value in a way that might be incorrect, and Rust doesn't deal in maybes:

```
let main_4 = Point2D {x: 25.0, y: 25.0};
let smaller;
{
    let main_5 = Point2D {x: 50.0, y: 50.0};
    smaller = smaller_x(&main_4, &main_5);
}
println!("The smaller x is {}", smaller);
```

This is a block expression between the { and the }, like we saw in Chapter 2, *Basics of the Rust Language*, which means it has its own scope, which owns the main_5 variable. That means that, when we create a borrow of main_5, it has a shorter lifetime than a borrow of the main_4 variable. Rust looks at the function definition for smaller_x and sees that the return value is only guaranteed valid within the lifetimes of both main_4 and main_5, so trying to use it after the block expression has ended produces a compiler error.

This is a compiler error even though *in fact* main_4 contains the smaller_x, and so the return value is a borrow of a value that will still be valid when we get to the print command. Rust doesn't analyze the logic of a function when it's checking lifetimes, it just looks at what we've told it about the parameters and return.

This is a good thing. In this case, it would have been possible to examine the values used for the parameters, recognize that they are constant values that will always result in the same behavior from the function, and logically reason out that the lifetime of the returned borrow is equal to the lifetime of the first parameter. However, in general, that sort of reasoning would not be possible (what if the first parameter was input by the user?), and attempting it would just cause problems. Imagine changing the source of a variable's value, and suddenly having compiler errors way off in some other part of the program that shouldn't care! It's better to have these things as a concrete part of a function's interface.

Ownership and the self parameter

As we've seen before, when we implement behavior for a type, the functions we define have `self`, `&self`, or `&mut self` as the first parameter. We now understand enough to recognize that that means that `self` is either moved (or copied) into the scope of the function, borrowed, or mutably borrowed. Which one we choose to use can have some pretty important consequences.

The data type of `self` is implicit: it's got to be the data type we're implementing the function on and, because of that, we don't get to specify the data type for `self` as part of the parameter list. Since there is no data type to prefix `&` or `&mut` to, we are allowed to write them before `self` instead.

In all three cases, `self` means *the data value that this function was called through*. If we have a `u32` variable named x and we tell Rust to `x.pow(3)`, the `pow` function implemented for `u32` will receive *two* parameters: the value of x as `self`, and 3 as the second parameter.

The same rules apply to moving, borrowing, and mutably borrowing the `self` value as they apply to any other value. If we currently have any borrows of a value, we can't mutably borrow it into `self`, nor can we move it (because that would invalidate the existing borrows). If we currently have a mutable borrow of the value, we can't borrow it or move it into `self`, because mutable borrows do not allow anyone else to borrow or change the value. Similarly, borrowing into a function's `self` affects how we can access the data in other places, because it *is* a borrow, and there are rules about how borrows coexist.

Moving self

If the `self` value is moved into the function, it's just like moving any other value; we can't continue to use it where it used to be anymore. Here is a function:

```
impl Point2D {
    pub fn transpose(self) -> Point2D {
        return Point2D {x: self.y, y: self.x};
    }
}
```

This can be said to *consume* the `self` value. The value is moved into the function's scope when it is called, and the old variable that used to contain the value is no longer usable. This particular function returns a new, different `Point2D` value, so the value of `self` is completely gone once this function is done running.

There are reasons why this might be exactly the behavior we want. In the previous example, the function transforms the `self` value into something new, which is reflected by having it consume the old value.

A very common use of functions that consume `self` is the **builder pattern**. This is a design pattern in Rust where we construct complex data structures bit by bit by filling in values to a builder structure, and then call a build function implemented on the builder structure to construct our final data value. Most of the time, the build function will consume its `self`, since each builder value should be used to construct only one final value.

 The builder pattern is essentially a way to use Rust's syntax to achieve the same things that are achieved by keyword arguments and default values in some other languages.

Any time the value of `self` will be invalidated by what the function does, either literally or conceptually, it makes sense to move `self` into the function's scope.

Borrowing self

If the `self` value is immutably borrowed into a function, then that function has read-only access to the value. This is useful in many situations, because it lets us call the function without making a copy of the `self` value for it to operate on, and without making the compiler ensure that the rules of write access are maintained.

Here's an example of a function that immutably borrows `self`:

```
impl Point2D {
    // ...
    pub fn magnitude(&self) -> f64 {
        return (self.x.powi(2) + self.y.powi(2)).sqrt();
    }
}
```

 This function returns $\sqrt{x^2 + y^2}$, or in other words, the distance between the point stored in `self` and the origin of the coordinate system.

The magnitude function doesn't need to change `self`, so there's no reason for it to use a mutable borrow and deal with the restrictions that implies. It could have worked with a moved `self`, but there's nothing wrong with calling the magnitude function twice on the same value, so that isn't what we want either.

Using an immutable borrow for `self` is most often the correct choice. We need a reason to use `self` or `&mut self`, and if we don't have such a reason, we use `&self`.

Mutably borrowing self

Sometimes, a function needs to change its `self`. For those situations, we can receive `self` as a mutable borrow with `&mut self`. Like any other time we create a mutable borrow, we can only call such a function if we have the value for `self` stored in a mutable variable, and that value is not currently borrowed anywhere else. In other words, we can only call functions that have write access to a value when we ourselves have write access to that value.

Here, we have an example function that mutable borrows `self`:

```
impl Point2D {
    // ...
    pub fn unit(&mut self) {
        let mag = self.magnitude();
        self.x = self.x / mag;
        self.y = self.y / mag;
    }
}
```

We see several things here. First, we are able to call the read-only `magnitude` function on `self`, even though that function takes its `self` as an immutable borrow, and we've got our `self` value as a mutable borrow. The reverse is not true: if we tried to call the `unit` function from inside of the `magnitude` function, the compiler would refuse to allow it.

Second, since we have write access to `self`, we can change the data stored in it. That's what write access means.

Third, we don't have a return type specified for this function. Technically, it defaults to returning `()`, but that's just another way of saying it doesn't return anything meaningful. It's common practice for functions that change `self` to not return a value or to return a `Result` with `()` as its success value if the function needs the ability to report errors. That's because the real result of the function is the updated `self` value.

Summary

Ownership is the thing that most separates Rust from other programming languages. It's an idea that seems obvious at first, then surprisingly complicated, and finally powerful and useful. Ownership gives Rust its nearly-free automatic memory management, along with things such as safe and easy multithreading and concurrency, and just generally being able to spot more errors in the compiler than other languages can.

Borrowing makes use of ownership to create a safe version of one of the biggest problem points for other languages: accessing data via a memory address. Mistakes with memory addresses are one of the most common problems programs encounter and, in Rust, those mistakes are caught by the compiler and reported along with helpful hints about how to address them.

In this chapter, we also looked at how to implement consuming, read-only, or read-write functions for data types, based on whether they move, borrow, or mutably borrow their `self` value, and discussed an assortment of errors that the compiler might report in various situations.

In the next chapter, we're going to learn about how to use pattern matching on data types to make decisions.

Making Decisions by Pattern Matching

4

We already saw Rust's `if` expressions, but those make decisions based on data values. Rust is a very type-conscious language, and so it's very important to be able to make decisions based on data types as well. Rust's `match` and `if let` expressions let us do that, comparing complex data types and allowing us to extract data values for further processing.

In this chapter, we're going to do the following:

- Learn how to use pattern matching in the context of variable assignment using the `let` statement
- Take what we've learned about pattern matching and apply it to decision making with the `if let` expression
- Use the `match` expression to choose exactly one of many possible patterns
- Use don't care values in pattern matching
- See how borrowing interacts with pattern matching
- Learn how to match complex, nested data structures

Variable assignment with pattern matching

We've seen many times how to assign a variable in Rust: we do something like `let x = y;`, which tells Rust to create a new variable named `x` and move or copy the value stored in `y` into it, as appropriate to the data type.

However, that's actually just a simplified case of what Rust is really doing, which is matching a pattern to a value and extracting data values from that matched pattern to store in the target variables, as in the following example:

```
pub struct DemoStruct {
 pub id: u64,
 pub name: String,
 pub probability: f64,
}
// ...
let source1 = DemoStruct { id: 31, name: String::from("Example Thing"),
probability: 0.42 };

let DemoStruct{ id: x, name: y, probability: z } = source1;
```

Okay, what just happened? First of all, we have a structure definition. We've seen those before, and the only new thing here is that we're using the `String` data type.

 `String` has an interesting relationship with `str`. When we're using `str`, we almost always actually use a borrow such as `&str` or `&'static str`, rather than plain `str`. That's because plain `str` doesn't have a fixed size in the stack, which makes a lot of the things we'd want to do impossible to compile. So, we use `&str` instead, which does have a fixed size. *But*, using a reference as a contained value in a data structure also opens the door to all sorts of lifetime-based restrictions, so we don't really want to use `pub name: &str` here. Fortunately, we can use `String` instead. `String` can masquerade as an `&str` when we need it to, but it's not actually a borrow, so the ownership is straightforward. It is, however, slightly less efficient to use, so the general rule is to use `String` when it solves a problem and use `&str` the rest of the time.

After that, we create a new data value with the `DemoStruct` type, with its three contained values. We've seen that before, too.

What on Earth are we doing in the last line of the example? `DemoStruct{ id: x, name: y, probability: z }` is a pattern. We're telling Rust that we expect the assigned value to be a `DemoStruct`, and that its contained values should in turn be matched with the x, y, and z sub-patterns.

When we use a variable name as a pattern, it matches any value and that value is assigned to that name, which is what is happening here. It's also what's happening with a simple `let x = 5`. So, x, y, and z end up being new variables containing the values that were previously stored in `source.id`, `source.name`, and `source.probability`, respectively.

We didn't have to use variable names for the sub-patterns, though. We could, for example, have tried this:

```
DemoStruct{ id: 31, name: y, probability: z } = source1;
```

If we do that, however, the compiler will report an error. The error is not because 31 is an invalid pattern. It's a perfectly good pattern and even happens to match the value we would actually find. The compiler will refuse to compile it, though, because it doesn't match all of the possibilities for the source value, and Rust doesn't allow `let` statements that might fail just because a variable's value got changed. Imagine of all the trouble that it could cause!

> The Rust compiler refers to being able to handle all of the possibilities when pattern matching as **covering**.

For patterns that might or might not match the input value, we can use `if let` expressions instead.

Using if let expressions to test whether a pattern matches

Using pattern matching to unpack values into multiple variables can be useful, but using pattern matching to make decisions is where this functionality really shines, as in the following example:

```
let source2 = DemoStruct { id: 35, name: String::from("Another Thing"),
probability: 0.42 };
let source3 = DemoStruct { id: 63, name: String::from("Super Thing"),
probability: 0.99 };
```

```
if let DemoStruct { id: 63, name: y, probability: z } = source2 {
    println!("When id is 63, name is {} and probability is {}", y, z);
}

if let DemoStruct { id: 63, name: y, probability: z } = source3 {
    println!("When id is 63, name is {} and probability is {}", y, z);
}
```

Here, we've defined two more variables containing `DemoStruct` values, and then used pattern matching to pull them back apart and assign their contained values to individual variables. This time, though, we did it in an `if let` expression instead of a `let` expression. That makes a world of difference, because now the pattern doesn't have to cover the whole domain of possible input values. If the pattern matches, the `if let` expression runs the code in its block. If the pattern doesn't match, then the `if let` expression doesn't run the code. It's conditional.

Since the pattern doesn't have to cover the domain, it means we can use `63` as a pattern to match against the `id` value, and there's nothing wrong with that. The same principle applies to more complex patterns or any pattern that only matches a subset of the values that might be represented by the data type it's matched against.

We can combine `if let` with normal `if` and `else` expressions, to create more complex decision-making structures, in a couple of ways.

First, we can put an `if let` expression inside the block of an `if`, `else if`, or `else` expression, and vice versa. That comes naturally, since there's nothing unusual about those block expressions—no special restrictions are placed on them just because they're inside a conditional expression.

Second, we can combine `if let` or `else if let` into the same chain of options as `if`, `else if`, and `else`. That looks like this:

```
    if false {
println!("This never happens");
}
else if let DemoStruct{ id: 35, name: y, probability: z } = source4 {
println!("When id is 35, name is {} and probability is {}", y, z);
}
else if let DemoStruct{ id: 36, name: y, probability: z } = source4 {
println!("When id is 36, name is {} and probability is {}", y, z);
}
else {
println!("None of the conditions matched");
}
```

The chain has to start with an `if` or `if let` expression (whichever one we need), and can then have any number of `else if` or `else if let`, and finally an `else if` expression we need one.

We're still just pulling data values out of our structures with the pattern matching, though. We can do more when the pattern is matched against other kinds of data type. An important one is the `Result` data type we've talked about previously. Remember that `Result` can be either `Ok` or `Err`, and either way it contains a value, either a result value or an error value of some sort. We saw before how to use the `?` or assorted functions to deal with `Result`, but we can also handle it with pattern matching, and that's often going to be the way we'll choose.

So, here's a function that constructs a `DemoStruct` value for us, but it only does it if the `id` value we ask for is even (the remainder when divided by two is zero). This function gives us a `Result` containing the created `DemoStruct` value or an error message:

```
pub fn might_fail(id: u64) -> Result<DemoStruct, &'static str> {
    if id % 2 == 0 {
      Ok(DemoStruct { id: id, name: String::from("An Even Thing"),
probability: 0.2})
   }
   else {
   Err("Only even numbers are allowed")
   }
}
```

If we then call that function, we can use pattern matching to figure out if it succeeded or failed:

```
if let Ok(x) = might_fail(37) {
    println!("Odd succeeded, name is {}", x.name);
}

if let Ok(x) = might_fail(38) {
    println!("Even succeeded, name is {}", x.name);
}
```

Here, we're calling `might_fail` twice, once with an odd number as the parameter value, and once with an even one. Both times, we use pattern matching to check whether the result is `Ok` and assign the contained value to a variable called `x` if it is.

`Ok` is not a data structure and neither is `Err`. We'll learn more about what they are in the next chapter. The point for now is that pattern matching gives us a simple way to check whether `Result` represents a success or a failure, and to handle one or both cases easily.

Using match to choose one of several patterns

You might have noticed in our previous example that we did not handle the case where the function returned an error value. In part, that's because handling that situation with `if let` is a little bit awkward. We could do this:

```
if let Ok(x) = might_fail(39) {
    println!("Odd succeeded, name is {}", x.name);
}
else if let Err(x) = might_fail(39) {
    println!("Odd failed, message is '{}'", x);
}
```

But that runs the function twice when it doesn't have to, so it's inefficient. We could fix that by doing this:

```
let result = might_fail(39);
if let Ok(x) = result {
    println!("Odd succeeded, name is {}", x.name);
}
else if let Err(x) = result {
    println!("Odd failed, message is '{}'", x);
}
```

That's better, but variables are for storing information and we don't really need the `result` value anymore once we've checked for the success or failure of the function, so there's no reason to keep storing it.

We can use a `match` expression for situations like this, for the best results:

```
match might_fail(39) {
    Ok(x) => { println!("Odd succeeded, name is {}", x.name) }
    Err(x) => { println!("Odd failed, message is '{}'", x) }
}
```

A `match` expression matches a single value (in this case, the result of calling `might_fail(39)`) against multiple patterns, until it finds a pattern that successfully matches the value, then runs the code block associated with that particular pattern. The patterns are matched from top to bottom so, normally, we put the most specific patterns first and the most generic patterns last.

Individual patterns in a `match` expression don't have to cover all of the possibilities for the value, but all of them together need to. If `Result` had three possibilities instead of two (

Ok, `Err`, and a hypothetical `Dunno`, for example), then our previous match expression would not compile, because we hadn't told it what to do in the case of `Dunno`.

That's a difference from a series of `if let` and `el`

se `if let`, which are free to ignore as many possibilities as they want. If we use `match`, the compiler will tell us if we've missed a possibility, so we should always use `match` when we intend to handle all of the options. On the other hand, `if let` is for cherry-picking one or a few special cases.

Using don't care in patterns

Sometimes, the trick that variable's names have of matching any value in a pattern would be useful, but we don't actually need the information that would be stored in the variable. For example, we might not care about the error value when matching `Result`, just the fact that there was an error. In that situation, we can use an _ symbol to indicate *I don't care what this value is*:

```
match might_fail(39) {
    Ok(x) => { println!("Odd succeeded, name is {}", x.name) }
    Err(_) => { println!("Odd failed! Woe is me.") }
}
```

That's the reason why _ by itself can not be used as a variable name: it has a special meaning of its own. We can match _ against any data value of any data type, even multiple times in the same expression, and the matched values will simply be ignored.

Matching a value to _ does not even move or copy the value. When we tell the compiler that we don't care about a value, it believes us. However, there's an intermediate level between a full variable and a *don't care*. If we start a variable name with an _ but continue on after that with a valid variable name, the named variable isn't a *don't care* but it *is* exempt from some compiler warnings.

For example, normally, the compiler would warn us if we received a value into a variable but then did nothing with it. Putting an _ at the start of the variable name means the compiler will not complain about that. Where _ by itself means *I don't care about this value*, starting a variable name with _ means *it's okay if I don't use this value*.

A common use for that is when we are designing for the future. We might anticipate that a function parameter or structure member will be useful in the future, so we put it in now, but don't use it yet. If we prefix the name with _, the compiler won't yell at us about it. Then, when the time comes to actually use it, we remove the _ so we benefit from all of the compiler's checks.

In the previous example, we used _ to match against the error value, meaning we don't care what the error value actually is, as long as it's an error. However, _ can match *anything*, which means we can also do this:

```
match might_fail(39) {
    Ok(x) => { println!("Odd succeeded, name is {}", x.name) }
    _ => { println!("If none of the above patterns match, _ certainly
will") }
}
```

Here, the last pattern in our `match` is an _, which matches anything while capturing no data at all. This is very much like putting `else` at the end of an `if` chain. Any match expression containing an _ pattern automatically covers the entire space of possible values, too, which means that, as long as there *is* a reasonable fallback action to take when none of the more precise patterns match, Rust won't complain to us that we're not covering all of the possibilities.

By the way, if we put a plain _ pattern anywhere but at the bottom of the `match` expression, Rust will warn us. This is a good thing, because any patterns under it will never, ever get a chance to match.

Moving and borrowing in pattern matches

When we match a pattern that contains variables, the matching data values are moved into the variables (unless their data type has the `Copy` trait). For example, this will cause the compiler to report an error, even though at first glance it seems reasonable, especially for people who are used to other programming languages:

```
let source5 = DemoStruct { id: 40, name: String::from("A Surprising
Thing"), probability: 0.93 };

if let DemoStruct {id: 41, name: x, probability: _} = source5 {
    println!("Extracted name: {}", x);
}

println!("source5.name is {}", source5.name);
```

The problem is that, after the `if let`, `source5.name` does not (or at least might not) contain a value anymore, because that value was moved to the `x` variable. The compiler can't be sure that the final `println!` command will always be valid, which is a problem because it happens whether the `if let` block gets run or not.

Can we borrow the value in `if let`, instead of moving it? That way, future uses of the value would still be valid. The answer is yes, but there's a problem we need to get a handle on. We can try this:

```
let source5 = DemoStruct { id: 40, name: String::from("A Surprising
Thing"), probability: 0.93 };

if let DemoStruct {id: 41, name: &x, probability: _} = source5 {
    println!("Extracted name: {}", x);
}

println!("source5.name is {}", source5.name);
```

But what we find is that the compiler complains that it expected `String` in the pattern, and found a reference instead. That's because using an `&` in the pattern this way doesn't mean we want to borrow the value; it means we expect the value to *already be a borrow* in the source data.

To tell Rust that we want to borrow a value that is matched by a variable in a pattern, we need to use a new keyword: `ref`. That looks like this:

```
let source5 = DemoStruct { id: 40, name: String::from("A Surprising
Thing"), probability: 0.93 };

if let DemoStruct {id: 41, name: ref x, probability: _} = source5 {
    println!("Extracted name: {}", x);
}

println!("source5.name is {}", source5.name);
```

At last, the compiler is happy, and so are we. The value in `source5.name` is not a borrow, but when we match `source5` to our pattern, we borrow it into the `x` variable, which means it is *not* moved out of `source5`, and the final `println!` will always work.

The `ref` keyword and the `&` symbol are closely related. These two lines of code do exactly the same thing:

```
let ref borrowed1 = source5;
let borrowed2 = &source5;
```

The difference between them is syntactic: we apply the `ref` keyword to the variable where the borrow *will be stored*, while we apply the `&` symbol to the variable where the value to be borrowed *is already stored*. We choose which one to use based on which end of the borrow we're writing, and we don't need both.

In fact, using both creates a borrow *of a borrow* of the original value, which is not usually what we want. The Rust compiler can automatically dereference any number of layers of borrowing in order to find the value it needs for a function parameter, so something like this works fine without causing any errors:

```
pub fn borrow_demostruct(x: &DemoStruct) {
    println!("Borrowed {}", x.name);
}

let ref borrowed_borrow = &source5;
borrow_demostruct(borrowed_borrow);
```

The compiler sees that the `borrow_demostruct` function wants a borrow of `DemoStruct`, and that the value we're trying to send it is a borrow of a borrow of a `DemoStruct`, so it dereferences that value once and passes that to the function parameter. Everything works.

What does a borrow of a borrow means? Well, first of all, we had a `DemoStruct` value. Then, we borrowed it, giving us an `&DemoStruct` value. Then, we borrowed *that* value, giving us an `&&DemoStruct` value.

However, the computer had to put in a little more effort than was necessary to achieve the same result. Multiple levels of borrowing should only be used when they solve a problem, because using them when we don't need them is just wasteful.

Also, `&&DemoStruct` is not actually the same data type as `&DemoStruct`, despite the fact that the Rust compiler can figure out how to treat the former as the latter when it's used as a function parameter. Sometimes, that matters.

Matching tuples and other more complex patterns

Matching simple patterns is very useful, but there's more that we can do. Patterns can be more complex, consisting of representations of several layers of nested data structures and other data types. Patterns can assign to a variable name while still looking deeper into the structure to make sure the contained information matches what we want. Or patterns can be simplified, checking only a few parts of the data structure and ignoring the rest.

Nested patterns

We can use pattern matching to pull a value out of a complex data structure. As long as the pattern matches the data value, it doesn't matter how complex the pattern and value are. If we want to match a tuple of tuples and extract one particular value from one of the inner tuples, we can do it like this:

```
let (_, (_, x, _, _), _) = ((5, 6, 7), (8, 9, 10, 11), (12, 13, 14, 15));
println!("x is {}", x);
```

This pattern matches any tuple of three elements, where the second element is a nested tuple of four elements, and stores the second element of that nested tuple in the x variable, then prints out the value of x.

We could have been even more specific, and replaced some of those _ with more detailed sub-patterns to match. That would have given us a pattern that paid more attention to the first and/or last elements out the outer tuple, or the other elements of the inner tuple.

We can use the same technique to dig into other data types, too; it's not limited to tuples. For example, earlier we used pattern matching to check whether a function had succeeded or failed to run properly:

```
match might_fail(39) {
    Ok(x) => { println!("Odd succeeded, name is {}", x.name) }
    Err(_) => { println!("Odd failed! Woe is me.") }
}
```

In that code, we just match the success value to the x variable, but what if we wanted to handle things differently depending on the details of the success value? We can do that by making the contained value match a more detailed sub-pattern:

```
match might_fail(38) {
    Ok(DemoStruct {id: 38, name: ref name, probability: _}) => {
        println!("Even succeeded with the proper id: name is {}", name)
    }
    Ok(DemoStruct {id: ref id, name: ref name, probability: _}) => {
        println!("Even succeeded with the wrong id: id is {}, name is {}",
id, name)
    }
    Err(_) => { println!("Even failed! Woe is me.") }
}
```

Here, we have a pattern that matches when the function returns a success *and* the success values is a DemoStruct with the proper ID, a second pattern that matches when the function return a success and the success value is a DemoStruct no matter what the ID is, and a third pattern that matches any error the function might return.

The first pattern matches the expected case. If it doesn't match, the second pattern matches, allowing us to deal with an unexpected result that is still technically reported as a success. If neither of those patterns match, the third one handles explicit errors.

If we compile this example, it works fine, but the compiler warns us that the name: in the first pattern and the id: and name: in the second pattern are redundant. That's because, when we are initializing a data structure or data structure pattern in Rust, we can leave out the destination name if it's the same as the source name. In other words, the second pattern could have been written like Ok(DemoStruct {ref id, ref name, probability: _}) and Rust still would have understood it, because id and name are the names of two of the structure's contained variables. The redundancy warning is just telling us that we wrote more than we needed to.

Storing a matched value and comparing it to a pattern

Normally, we either use a variable name to match part of a data value, or we use a structural pattern to check that it's the right "shape" and use variable names inside that structural pattern to match and extract the parts of it we're interested in.

We can do both at the same time, though, by using the @ symbol:

```
if let (1, x @ (_, _), _) = (1, (2, 3), (4, 5, 6)) {
    println!("matched x to {:?}", x);
}
```

So, here we have a pattern that matches a 3-tuple that has 1 as its first item, a 2-tuple as its second item, and anything as its third item, and stores the second item (which it has confirmed is a 2-tuple) in a variable called x. The variable name to store into came before the @, and the pattern to check the match against came after.

Ignoring most of a data structure

Some data structures contains a great many data values, and it would be inconvenient to have to go through and list each one of them in each pattern we want to match against. Fortunately, Rust has a shorthand syntax that means *everything else is a don't care.*

To do that, we can include .. at the end of the pattern, like so:

```
if let DemoStruct {id: 40, ..} = source5 {
    println!("id is 40, don't care about the rest");
}
```

That has the same effect as listing out all of the structure's contained variables, *except* the ones we've explicitly described in the pattern, and matching each one to an _.

Gotchas

There are some seemingly reasonable things we might try to do with pattern matching that don't work as we might expect. We're going to take a look at those, and work out what they're actually doing and why Rust works that way.

Not all values can be matched against a literal pattern

In all of our examples so far, when we matched `DemoStruct` in a pattern, we matched `probability` to a variable or to _. That's because `probability` is a floating point number, which means that two values that are functionally identical might not compare as exactly equal.

If we try to use a floating-point literal in a pattern (in Rust 1.29), we see a warning like this:

```
warning: floating-point types cannot be used in patterns
  --> src/main.rs:127:61
    |
127 |         Ok(DemoStruct {id: 38, name: ref name, probability: 57.3}) => {
    |                                                              ^^^^
    |
    = note: #[warn(illegal_floating_point_literal_pattern)] on by default
    = warning: this was previously accepted by the compiler but is being phased out; it will become a hard error in a future release!
    = note: for more information, see issue #41620 <https://github.com/rust-lang/rust/issues/41620>
```

It's just a warning but, as the warning says, it's going to become an error as Rust evolves. We should treat it as an error, regardless, because the pattern will likely not work properly even though it (currently) compiles.

The reason for that, in this case, is that floating point numbers are approximate. They have to fit into a finite number of bits, so they have to be rounded sometimes. That can result in numbers that should be identical in a purely mathematical sense being different because their representations differ in the least significant bits. The least significant bits usually make such a tiny difference that rounding errors don't much matter, but they can throw off an equality comparison.

The upshot is that if we try to use a literal in a pattern that isn't safe to use, Rust will warn us or give us an error. As usual, Rust isn't willing to let a potential problem go unremarked.

If we need to do something like this, we can use match guards to work around the limitation. We're about to learn about them, so keep reading!

Patterns assign values to variable names

When we use a variable name in a pattern, it matches any value and the matched value is stored in the variable. That means that if we were to try this:

```
let x = 5;
let source6 = DemoStruct {id: 7, name: String::from("oops"), probability:
0.26};
if let DemoStruct { id: x, name: _, probability: _ } = source6 {
    println!("The pattern matched, x is {}", x);
}
```

We do not get a pattern that compares the source6.id value to the value of x (five in this case), we don't get what we expect.

Instead, we get an error saying that the pattern is irrefutable:

```
error[E0162]: irrefutable if-let pattern
  --> src/main.rs:138:12
   |
138 |        if let DemoStruct { id: x, name: _, probability: _ } = source6 {
   |               ^^^^^^^^^^^^^^^^^^^^^^^^^^^^^^^^^^^^^^^^^^^^^^^ irrefutable pattern

error: aborting due to previous error

For more information about this error, try `rustc --explain E0162`.
error: Could not compile `chapter04`.

To learn more, run the command again with --verbose.
```

 Irrefutable means the pattern will never fail to match, which is a problem in an if let expression.

If we try a similar pattern that it is refutable, but still uses the x variable, the program compiles, but the pattern matches when we didn't want it to:

```
let x = 5;
let source6 = DemoStruct {id: 7, name: String::from("oops"), probability:
0.26};
if let DemoStruct { id: 7, name: x, probability: _ } = source6 {
    println!("The pattern matched, x is {}", x);
}
```

Both of these situations arise because of a rule we already talked about: variable names used in patterns match any value, and store the matched value into a new variable with the given name. If we think about it, that implies that if there's already a variable with that name, its current value doesn't matter.

That doesn't mean we're entirely out of luck, though. We can use an extension of the match syntax to involve existing variables in the decision:

```
let x = 5;
let source7 = DemoStruct {id: 7, name: String::from("oops"), probability:
0.26};
match source7 {
    DemoStruct { id: y, name: _, probability: _ } if y == x => {
        println!("The pattern with match guard matched, y is {}", y);
    }
    _ => {
        println!("The pattern with match guard did not match")
    }
}
```

What we're doing here is applying a **match guard** to the pattern. We do that by putting the if keyword after the pattern, but before the =>, and following it up with a Boolean expression. This lets us add non-pattern matching criteria to a match branch. In this case, we're saying that if the pattern matches and the ID (stored in y) matches the value stored in x, we should run that block of code.

 There has been talk of creating a similar feature for if let, but mostly people just use nested if expressions or match.

When we use a match guard, we need to be especially careful that our pattern doesn't shadow any variable names we want to use in the guard. That's why, in this example, we matched the id of DemoStruct to a variable named y instead of x. We needed to keep x around so our match guard could use it.

Summary

In this chapter, we've seen how to use pattern patching to enhance our ability to make decisions and assign variables. In particular, we've learned the following:

- How to assign *part* of a data value to a variable by matching the whole value to a pattern that matches the part we're interested in to a variable name
- How to use `if let` and `else if let` to decide whether a particular branch of an `if` chain should run
- How to use `match` to check a single value against multiple patterns
- How to use _ as a *don't care* in patterns
- The difference between a pattern that matches a borrowed value and a pattern that borrows a matched value
- How to match patterns for complex, nested data structures
- Surprises that can arise when we use pattern matching, and how to deal with them

We'll be seeing more pattern matching in the next chapter, when we look at enumerations, traits, and trait objects.

5
One Data Type Representing Multiple Kinds of Data

Sometimes, a data value might need to be one of multiple different data types. Rust has three ways of addressing that situation without breaking strict type safety: enumerations, trait objects, and `Any`. Each approach has strengths and weaknesses, so we'll examine them all and talk about when each is appropriate.

In this chapter, we're going to learn about the following:

- What an enumeration is
- How to create an enumeration type
- How to create enumeration values
- How to use the information stored in an enumeration value
- What a trait and a trait object are
- How to create a trait
- How to create a trait object
- How to use a trait object
- What `Any` is
- How to use `Any`
- What enumerations are good for, what trait objects are good for, and what `Any` is good for

Enumerations

Like structures, enumerations allow us to establish a new data type. The content is different from a structure, though. When we say that the data type of a variable is an enumeration, we're telling Rust that its contained value is required to be one of the specific choices we've described for that enumeration and can't be anything else.

Basic enumerations

In Rust, an enumeration is a data type representing one of a fixed set of values. For example, we could define an enumeration of the commonly recognized seven colors of the rainbow, as shown here:

```
pub enum Color {
    Red,
    Orange,
    Yellow,
    Green,
    Blue,
    Indigo,
    Violet,
}
```

Once we define this enumeration, we can use `Color` as a data type and `Color::Red` or the like as data values of that type:

```
let color: Color = Color::Green;
```

An enumeration is created with the `enum` keyword. Notice that, like a structure, an enumeration needs the `pub` keyword if we want it to be directly accessible outside the current module. Between the { and }, we have the list of possible values for the data type, listed by name and separated by commas.

Rust is somewhat opinionated about capitalization, so it will warn us if any of the enumeration values start with a lowercase letter, though that is not actually an error.

Parameterized enumerations

Okay, so what do enumerations have to do with representing different kinds of data in one variable? Well, there's one more feature that enumeration values can have that changes everything: parameters.

Imagine we wanted to create a representation of a sequence of driving directions, such as *turn right, forward three blocks,* or *stop.* This example is simple enough that we could probably get by with a simple enumeration, but even this will be easier with parameters:

```
pub enum Drive {
    Forward(u8),
    Turn{slight: bool, right: bool},
    Stop,
}
```

What we have here is an enumeration with parameterized values. The Forward value has a u8 parameter (unsigned 8 bit integer), while the Turn value has two bool parameters with names. Stop doesn't need any parameters.

Essentially, the Forward value carries a 1-tuple along with it, while the Turn value carries along a structure with two members. That's why parentheses are used around the Forward parameter and braces are used around the Turn parameters. Whether we want the parameters to be tuple-like or structure-like is our decision to make. Either way, we can have as many or as few parameters as we need.

Now, we can create a variable of the Drive type, and it might contain a Forward, Turn, or Stop parameter. If it's a Forward parameter, that means the variable also contains a u8 number telling us how far to drive. If it's a Turn parameter, that means the variable also contains a pair of Boolean values that tell us whether to turn right or left, and whether or not the turn is slight. In other words, the variable might contain any one of several different kinds of information.

If you're familiar with C++, or a similar language, keep in mind that Rust enumerations are not very much like C++ enumerations. A Rust enumeration with parameterized values is more like a C++ union, except it's type checked and safe.

Better still, we can create an array of driving instructions, to represent a complete journey:

```
let directions = [
    Drive::Forward(3),
    Drive::Turn{slight: false, right: true},
    Drive::Forward(1),
    Drive::Stop,
];
```

This array of Drive values represents driving forward three blocks, turning right, driving forward one more block, and stopping.

Checking the value type and extracting parameter values

When the program runs, it can take different actions depending on the specific enumeration type it's looking at, and it has access to the data values that were stored as parameters. We've already seen the best tool for doing that, match:

```
for step in directions.iter() {
    match step {
        Drive::Forward(blocks) => {
            println!("Drive forward {} blocks", blocks);
        },
        Drive::Turn{slight, right} => {
            println!("Turn {}{}",
                        if *slight {
                            "slightly "
                        }
                        else {
                            ""
                        },
                        if *right {
                            "right"
                        }
                        else {
                            "left"
                        }
            );
        },
        Drive::Stop => {
            println!("You have reached your destination");
        }
    };
};
```

Here, we have a for loop that processes each item in our array of directions, one at a time, starting with the first one. Step by step, here's what is going on:

1. We asked directions to provide us with an iterator, which it's happy to do. The iterator will give us a borrow of each value contained in the array, one at a time.
2. The for loop requests a value from the iterator, and assigns the returned borrow to a variable called step.

3. The match expression uses the `step` variable to provide the value that it will match against. Because that variable changes each time the loop goes through, the match expression compares against a different value each time:
   - If the `step` variable contains (a borrow of) `Drive::Forward`, its parameter is assigned to the variable named `blocks`. Because `step` *is* a borrow, the value in `blocks` is a borrow as well, but, in this instance that doesn't make a significant difference. We pass it on to `println!`, which calls a function on it to turn it into a text string, which in turn, dereferences it automatically.
   - If the `step` variable contains (a borrow of) `Drive::Turn`, borrows of its parameters are assigned to the `slight` and `right` names, and we can use the shorthand notation we've seen before for that because `slight` and `right` are the names of the variables in both the source and the destination. Then comes a print command, but we're using `if` expressions to decide exactly what to print. Notice that we have explicitly dereferenced the `slight` and `right` values; they *are* borrows and, unlike when we call functions, `if` expressions don't automatically dereference for us, we need to do it ourselves.
   - If the `step` variable contains (a borrow of) `Drive::Stop`, there are no parameters to deal with and we just print out a message.
4. If there are any values left in the iterator, got back to step 2.

Pretty cool. We've got some code here that does something kind of real. That's when the fun really starts!

Result is an enumeration, accessed via the prelude

You may have noticed already, but the `Result` type with its `Ok` and `Err` values looks an awful lot like an enumeration. That's because it is an enumeration, which is how it's able to contain different data types depending on whether it represents an error or a success. It's an enumeration with generic type parameters, so we won't be able to pull off quite the same functionality until we learn about those but, at its base, it's still just an enumeration.

We can use `Ok` and `Err` instead of `Result::Ok` and `Result::Err` when we write functions that might fail or handle the results of such functions, because those values are added directly to the Rust *prelude* for our convenience. Actually, we can use the `Result` type without saying where it came from for the same reason.

The prelude is a collection of very basic and useful data types, values, and traits that is automatically made available in every Rust module. It contains such things as String, Vec (a *vector*, which has the same relation to arrays that String does to str), and Box (which we'll talk about in the next chapter).

Traits and trait objects

Trait objects are another mechanism Rust has for storing a data value that might be one of several possible types into a single variable, but before we can talk about trait objects, we need to talk about traits.

Traits

A trait is a name and formal definition for a specific bit of functionality that a data type may provide. Previously, we've talked about how data types might have the Copy trait, and how, when they do, the compiler copies them instead of moving them. That is the general idea: when a trait is implemented for a data type, that data type gains the ability to interact with the rest of the program in some specific way.

 Some of the built-in traits, such as Copy, actually affect how the *compiler* interacts with the type, but we're more interested in creating our own traits here. We'll talk about those built-in traits in a later chapter.

That's all very abstract, so let's get more concrete by looking at the same "driving directions" problem that we previously solved with an enumeration. We still want to be able to have an array of driving instructions, and print them out in order, so let's create a trait that represents the ability to print out a driving instruction:

```
pub trait PrintableDirection {
    fn forward(&self);
    fn reverse(&self);
}
```

The trait keyword introduces a trait, unsurprisingly. Inside of it, we have the signatures of the functions that make up the *interface* of this trait. In other words, if a data type is going to have the PrintableDirection trait, it needs to provide implementations of these functions that are specialized for that type and trait.

It's possible for one data type to have multiple implemented functions with the same name, as long as each of those functions is part of a different trait. Traits don't need to worry about name collisions with other traits or the basic data type.

We've expanded the functionality beyond what we did with enumerations, by specifying that a data value that has the `PrintableDirection` trait knows how to print itself out in both the *going to* and *coming from* directions of travel—or, at least, that's what we intend for the `forward` and `reverse` functions to mean.

Traits can specify functions by just providing a signature, as before, or they can also provide a default implementation of the function, by simply filling in a complete function definition instead. When the trait is implemented for a particular data type, functions with default implementations do not have to be implemented, though they can be, if necessary.

Notice that the function signatures inside the trait do not have the `pub` keyword. The trait itself is public or not, as a whole. In this case (and most cases), the trait is public, so the functions that it requires are automatically public.

Implementing our PrintableDirection trait

Traits don't exist independently; they are something that data types have. So, the first thing we need to do is create data types to represent the various kinds of driving directions:

```
pub struct Forward {
    pub blocks: u8,
}

pub struct Turn {
    pub slight: bool,
    pub right: bool,
}

pub struct Stop {}
```

We're just using basic structures here, but traits can be implemented for *any* data type.

These structures contain the same information that we included in the enumeration parameters before. The Stop structure is interesting, because it's empty. It stores no information at all. Its only purpose is to be a data type.

Now, we have a trait and we have data types, but so far they are not related in any way. Let's implement our trait for each of these types:

```
impl PrintableDirection for Forward {
    fn forward(&self) {
        println!("Go forward {} blocks", self.blocks);
    }

    fn reverse(&self) {
        println!("Go forward {} blocks", self.blocks);
    }
}

impl PrintableDirection for Turn {
    fn forward(&self) {
        println!("Turn {}{}",
                if self.slight {"slightly "} else {""},
                if self.right {"right"} else {"left"});
    }

    fn reverse(&self) {
        println!("Turn {}{}",
                if self.slight {"slightly "} else {""},
                if self.right {"left"} else {"right"});
    }
}

impl PrintableDirection for Stop {
    fn forward(&self) {
        println!("You have reached your destination");
    }

    fn reverse(&self) {
        println!("Turn 180 degrees");
    }
}
```

These implementation blocks look similar to the ones we've seen before, but this time instead of just saying `impl` and the type name, they say to implement the trait for the type name. Then, inside of it, we place the specific versions of the trait's functions that apply to that data type.

The `Forward`, `Turn`, and `Stop` data types now each have the `PrintableDirection` trait, which means that each of them knows how to display the information it contains as a driving instruction.

Trait objects

`Forward`, `Turn`, and `Stop` are still three different data types. There's no data type that represents *Forward, Turn, Stop,* and though we could create one using an enumeration, there's another way. There is a data type that represents a borrow of *any* data type that has the `PrintableDirection` trait. It's written as `&dyn PrintableDirection` and is called a trait object reference.

We *can't* just write something like `let x: dyn PrintableDirection` and create a variable that can store anything with the `PrintableDirection` trait. It needs to be a borrow, or something that stores contained data outside the stack, such as the `Box` type we'll look at in the next chapter.

The `dyn` keyword is short for *dynamic dispatch,* and it means that what looks and acts like a borrow in most ways is actually a little more complicated. The memory address stored in the borrow itself is actually the address of a hidden data structure.

That hidden data structure contains the actual borrow address and the memory addresses of the functions that implement the trait for the borrowed data value. When we assign a data value to a trait object, Rust initializes that hidden data structure, and when we call one of the trait functions, Rust looks up which function to actually call in the same hidden data structure.

That means that calling a function through a trait object will always have a few extra steps that the computer needs to perform, compared to calling a function on a data value with a concrete type. On the other hand, if we think about it, any mechanism that could possibly allow us to work with arbitrary data types has to allocate time and memory for keeping track of what kind of data it's working with and where the data value is stored. If we tried to create the same functionality from scratch, we'd end up doing the same thing.

Using our PrintableDirection trait

So, instead of an array of enumeration values, this time we're going to create an array of trait object references:

```
let mut directions = [
    &Forward{ blocks: 5 },
    &Turn{ slight: true, right: false },
    &Forward{ blocks: 1 },
    &Turn{ slight: false, right: true },
    &Forward{ blocks: 2 },
    &Stop{},
];
```

Unfortunately, if we try to compile that, we get an error, as shown here:

```
error[E0308]: mismatched types
  --> src/traitobjs.rs:54:9
   |
54 |         &Turn{ slight: true, right: false },
   |         ^^^^^^^^^^^^^^^^^^^^^^^^^^^^^^^^^^^ expected struct `traitobjs::Forward`, found struct `traitobjs::Turn`
   |
   = note: expected type `&traitobjs::Forward`
              found type `&traitobjs::Turn`

error: aborting due to previous error

For more information about this error, try `rustc --explain E0308`.
error: Could not compile `chapter05`.
```

This time, Rust can't figure out the data type of the array just by looking at the value we're assigning to it, because that value looks like an array containing multiple data types, which is not something we can even do in Rust. The compiler is not going to go looking for traits they all implement, pick one arbitrarily, and decide that the array is actually an array of trait objects. That would be bad more often than it was helpful, so we have to tell Rust what data type the directions variable should have.

What we actually tell it is that `directions` is `[&dyn PrintableDirection; 6]`. That means that it's an array of `PrintableDirection` trait object references and has room for six of them. Now, the compiler knows how to correctly interpret our array expression:

```
let mut directions: [&dyn PrintableDirection; 6] = [
    &Forward{ blocks: 5 },
    &Turn{ slight: true, right: false },
    &Forward{ blocks: 1 },
    &Turn{ slight: false, right: true },
    &Forward{ blocks: 2 },
    &Stop{},
];
```

Now, we're ready to actually print out the driving directions:

```
for step in directions.iter() {
    step.forward();
};
```

Just for fun, we'll also print out the directions for returning home:

```
directions.reverse();

for step in directions.iter() {
    step.reverse();
};
```

There are two function calls to reverse here, and *they're not calling the same function*. The `directions.reverse()` call is calling a reverse function implemented on arrays, which reverses the order of the items stored in the array. Meanwhile, the `step.reverse()` call is calling the reverse function, which all types that have the `PrintableDirection` trait must implement, as appropriate for the specific concrete type of the step value. These functions happen to have the same name, but they're not at all the same thing.

When we compile and run all of the trait object code, we get output like this:

```
Trait object-style driving directions:
Go forward 5 blocks
Turn slightly left
Go forward 1 blocks
Turn right
Go forward 2 blocks
You have reached your destination
Turn 180 degrees
Go forward 2 blocks
Turn left
Go forward 1 blocks
Turn slightly right
Go forward 5 blocks
```

Yay, it works!

Trait objects only provide access to the trait interface

When we use a trait object, the *only* parts of the original object that we have access to are the parts that are defined by the trait. That means that we can call the `forward` and `reverse` functions, but we have no direct access to the `blocks` member of the `Forward` type, or the `slight` member of the `Turn` type, and so on. A trait object only gives us the things that are guaranteed to be present in *any* of the data types it can represent: the trait's own interface.

That makes sense, when we think about it. What's the computer supposed to do if we ask it to access `slight`, but the value we're looking at is actually a `Forward` type? Some languages would let us try and just crash the program if we tried it at the wrong time, while others would spend time while the program was running checking things like that and catching errors as they happen, but neither of those is the Rust way. In Rust, if the compiler can't be sure that something is okay, it's usually an error.

That means that a trait's interface needs to be complete, in the sense that anything you can reasonably do with a data value that has the trait should be part of the interface. That's not a burden most of the time. After all, why would we want it any other way?

 We've been using the word **interface** a lot. Some languages, such as Java, have a feature that's actually *called* interface, and yes, Rust traits are similar to Java interfaces, although not identical.

Any

`Any` is a trait that most data types in Rust implement automatically, which means we can store almost anything in a trait object of `Any` type. However, as we've mentioned before, we can only access the stored value in a trait object in terms of that trait's interface, so what does the `Any` interface let us do?

Any can store almost anything

The Rust compiler automatically implements `Any` for any data type, *unless* that data type contains non-static references. So, our `Forward`, `Turn`, and `Stop` structures that we used in the trait objects section already automatically implement `Any`, but something like this would not:

```
pub struct DoesNotHaveAnyTrait<'a> {
    pub name: &'a str,
    pub count: i32,
}
```

More accurately, `DoesNotHaveAnyTrait` only has the `Any` trait when `'a` is equal to `'static`, which it is if we use a simple string expression such as `this is a static string` to initialize it, but not if we use some other mechanism for retrieving or constructing an `&str` value.

The error the compiler will give if we try something impossible along these lines will probably be about lifetimes rather than explicitly about the `Any` trait, as in the following example:

```
error[E0597]: `wrong` does not live long enough
  --> src/any.rs:25:37
   |
25 |         &DoesNotHaveAnyTrait{ name: wrong.as_str(), count: 16},
   |                                     ^^^^^ borrowed value does not live long enough
...
60 | }
   | - borrowed value only lives until here
   |
   = note: borrowed value must be valid for the static lifetime...
```

Do you see the note? The code that caused the error was trying to create an &dyn Any, which told the compiler that the 'a lifetime needed to be compatible with 'static, which told it that the lifetime of wrong.as_str() was too short, so it reported an error.

Usually, that's not much of a problem, because we have several other reasons to avoid using non-static references in our data types, and we can use String, Vec, Box, and the like to achieve the same result. It's just something to keep in mind.

But to access it we have to already know about the real data type

Getting back to our example, we'll create our array of driving directions, and we'll add a something else that isn't a driving direction, just to prove that we can.

Here, we have an array of Any trait references containing driving directions and one other thing:

```
use std::any::Any;

//...

pub struct DoesHaveAnyTrait {
 pub name: String,
 pub count: i32,
}

//...

let okay = String::from("okay");

let directions: [&dyn Any; 7] = [
    &Forward{ blocks: 5 },
    &Turn{ slight: true, right: false },
    &Forward{ blocks: 1 },
    &Turn{ slight: false, right: true },
    &Forward{ blocks: 2 },
    &Stop{},
    &DoesHaveAnyTrait{ name: okay, count: 16},
];
```

So far, it looks rather similar to our trait object example, which makes sense since `Any` is a trait too, and this is still an array of trait object references. The huge difference here is that we've added one more item to the array, and it doesn't have anything at all to do with driving directions.

Trait object references only give us access to the trait's functions. Now that we've got an array of `Any` trait object references, what functions does `Any` provide that let us do something useful? `Any` gives us two important functions: there is a function that checks whether the contained value has a particular data type, and there is a family of functions that lets us extract the contained value.

For a first example, we'll look at the function that allows us to check the data type:

```
for step in directions.iter() {
    if step.is::<Forward>() {
        println!("Go forward");
    }
    else if step.is::<Turn>() {
        println!("Turn here");
    }
    else if step.is::<Stop>() {
        println!("Stop now");
    }
}
```

There's some new syntax here. When we say `step.is::<Forward>()`, we're saying that we want to call the `is` function that was defined within the (automatically created) `impl Any for Forward` implementation. The compiler knows we're talking about `Any` because `step` is an `&dyn Any`, but it wouldn't know we wanted the `Forward` version rather than one of the countless other implementations of `Any` for specific types, so we needed to tell it.

 This syntax is a little confusing, since it's backwards from what we would write in a `use` statement, but it otherwise looks similar. It does read well, though: *if step is forward* almost works as a sentence.

This version is a little unsatisfying, though, because the printout is entirely based on the data type, without taking into account the information stored in the data values. We could do just as well with an unparameterized enumeration. Fortunately, we can also use the downcast functions of `Any` to get access to the referenced value:

```
for step in directions.iter() {
    if let Some(x) = step.downcast_ref::<Forward>() {
        x.forward();
    }
```

```
    else if let Some(x) = step.downcast_ref::<Turn>() {
        x.forward();
    }
    else if let Some(x) = step.downcast_ref::<Stop>() {
        x.forward();
    }
}
```

Once again, we're telling Rust that we want to call the versions of the Any functions that come from specific type implementations of that trait. In the first if let branch, we're asking Any to give us a reference to a Forward data value. If the value actually *is* a Forward data value, that function will return an enumeration value called Some, which has the reference as its parameter. If the value *is not* a Forward data value, the function will return an enumeration value called None, which naturally does not match the if let pattern.

> Some and None are the two possible values of the Option enumeration, which is another thing included in the prelude. It is used widely to represent data values that might or might not exist, especially when they are not required to exist. It's common in other languages to have a special value such as NULL, null, None, or nil, which can be assigned to anything. Rust's None can only be assigned to Option, which helps the compiler ensure that everything is correct.

The x variables in this example are actual references to Forward, Turn, or Stop data values, respectively, and so if we make it into the code block for one of the if branches, we have access to everything that it is possible to do with that data type, not just the features defined by a particular trait. In fact, we're calling the forward functions implemented in the PrintableDirection trait for those types, which is a pretty good demonstration that we have full access.

Notice that, with both is and downcast_ref, there's no way to use them without specifying which concrete data type we're interested in. If we try to use those functions without specifying exactly which data type to use, we get an error like this:

```
error[E0282]: type annotations needed
  --> src/any.rs:32:17
   |
32 |         if step.is() {
   |                 ^^ cannot infer type for `T`

error: aborting due to previous error

For more information about this error, try `rustc --explain E0282`.
error: Could not compile `chapter05`.
```

That means that while `Any` can be used to store almost anything, we can't access the stored information unless we explicitly handle the correct data type for the stored value. In our example, we didn't have an if branch to handle `DoesHaveAnyTrait` values, so the last value in the array ended up being ignored.

 In addition to `downcast_ref`, the `Any` trait also provides `downcast_mut`, which gives us a mutable reference. In some circumstances, a `downcast` function is also available, which moves the value into our current scope instead of borrowing it.

Comparison of these techniques

The Rust community tends to prefer using enumerations to address one-variable-multiple-types problems. In terms of runtime cost, a simple enumeration is maximally efficient, and efficiency is important to Rust programmers.

However, there is a downside to using enumerations, which is that the `match` expressions (or similar) that decide how to handle a particular enumeration value and associated data might be spread throughout the source code of the program. If we discover a need to add or remove an enumeration value, or change an enumeration value's parameters, we have to find and change every one of those match expressions.

If we decide to add a `Reverse` value to the `Drive` enumeration, the match expressions have to be changed:

```
error[E0004]: non-exhaustive patterns: `&Reverse` not covered
 --> src/enums.rs:31:15
    |
31 |          match step {
    |                ^^^^ pattern `&Reverse` not covered

error: aborting due to previous error

For more information about this error, try `rustc --explain E0004`.
error: Could not compile `chapter05`.
```

The compiler will point out each `match` expression that needs to be updated, but it won't catch places where an `if let` expression would need similar changes (because `if let` is allowed to handle only some of the possibilities), so this can be a significant problem.

Trait objects on the other hand let us keep all the related code close together, by making the behavior for different data types actually be part of the data type. They also allow us to write code that works with data types we haven't even created yet, but they are less efficient, because the computer needs to maintain and use the hidden trait object structure while the program is running.

We might think we could get the best of both worlds by creating an enumeration and then implementing functions on it that contain match expressions and handle each of the enumeration values differently, and to an extent, we can. However, if those functions work by picking another enumeration value-specific function and calling *that*, we've just recreated trait objects all over again, but less efficiently.

If we try something like the following to avoid trait objects, we're better off just using trait objects:

```
pub enum LikeATraitObject {
    Integer(i32),
    Float(f32),
    Bool(bool),
}

fn handle_integer(x: i32) {
    println!("Integer {}", x);
}

fn handle_float(x: f32) {
    println!("Float {}", x);
}

fn handle_bool(x: bool) {
    println!("Bool {}", x);
}

impl LikeATraitObject {
    pub fn handle(&self) {
        match self {
            LikeATraitObject::Integer(x) => { handle_integer(*x); }
            LikeATraitObject::Float(x) => { handle_float(*x); }
            LikeATraitObject::Bool(x) => { handle_bool(*x); }
        }
    }
}
```

That's not to say that such constructions are useless, because they're not. However, if the *only* reason for doing something like that is to avoid using trait object references, it's a mistake.

It may seem like `Any` is actually the best option, since it can store such a wide range of values *and* gives us full access to the stored value data, but usually one of the other choices is better. Using `Any` means we need to check for all of the possibilities in various places throughout the code, as we would with an enumeration and, unlike an enumeration, the compiler can't give us any help at all in finding places that need to change because, like a trait object reference, there's no defined list of possibilities. `Any` is, in many ways, the worst of both worlds.

There are *some* problems that `Any` is the right choice for, though. If we really need to handle a collection of unrelated data types, we need `Any`.

Summary

Okay, so we have three different ways to approach the same problem, each with different strengths and weaknesses:

- We learned that enumerations are the most efficient, especially for simple cases
- We learned that trait object references produce the simplest code, at the cost of additional overhead
- We learned that the `Any` trait gives us a way to refer to almost anything, but we have to explicitly extract the type of information we need

In the next chapter, we're going to learn how to store data outside the stack, and why we would want to.

6
Heap Memory and Smart Pointers

We've talked about the stack, and how it is the place where Rust stores data and keeps track of what needs to be kept around and what needs to be cleaned up. It's a powerful, useful mechanism, but it's not right for everything.

Imagine we have a variable that contains an image. It takes up several megabytes of memory, and we need to transfer ownership of it between various parts of our program at different times. If we just put it on the stack, and allow Rust to move it into new scopes as needed, everything will work, but it will be slowed down by the need to copy those megabytes of data every time it moves the value to a new owner.

That's not the only scenario where storing information on the stack isn't ideal, but it's a good illustration.

On the other hand, the last thing we want to do is to break the stack and scope-based ownership model, which gives Rust so much of its power.

Fortunately, there's a way to store data outside of the stack, and still have it act as though it were part of a scope: smart pointers.

The Rust standard library includes several different kinds of smart pointer, meant to address different needs. Smart pointer values themselves are stored in the stack, just like other data values are, but they include the necessary instrumentation to allocate a chunk of *heap* memory when they are created, and release it back to the system when their lifetimes end. A data value stored in that heap memory can be accessed through the smart pointer, as if it was stored inside the smart pointer.

The **heap** is the counterpoint to the stack. Where the stack has a specific structure that helps Rust keep track of which operations are safe and which are not at any given time, the heap can be thought of as unorganized memory. In general, a program can ask for a section of heap memory to be reserved for use at any time, and can release it back to the system at any time. Now imagine what happens when a section of heap memory is allocated too late, or released too soon, or not released when it should be. Mistakes with memory allocation and deallocation are one of the main reasons programs crash.

Thanks to smart pointers, the lifetime of values stored in heap memory mirror the lifetimes of values that follow Rust's normal rules, but with the big advantage that the section of heap memory does not have to be copied when the smart pointer is moved to a new scope. Our multi-megabyte image can be moved around between scopes for the cost of moving a few bytes, because the image itself does not have to move, just the smart pointer that controls it.

Box

The most straightforward of the standard smart pointers is the Box. A Box does what we've been discussing so far: it stores a data value on the heap, while ensuring that it still follows the lifetime rules as if it were actually part of the Box value itself.

Here's an example. First, we'll create a data type for the data we want to store on the heap:

```
pub struct Person {
    pub name: String,
    pub validated: bool,
}
```

Now, creating and using the Box itself is easy:

```
let jack = Box::new(Person { name: "Jack".to_string(), validated: true });
let x = &jack.name;
println!("The person in the box is {}", x);
```

The first line creates a Box. We have to give it a data value to store, because one thing Rust is not okay with is an empty Box, so we initialize a Person object and pass it to the function, which creates a new Box to be used as its internal value.

Why does Rust not allow an empty `Box`, or any other kind of smart pointer, for that matter? Because if it did, then it would have to worry about whether a given smart pointer referred to initialized memory or not whenever that smart pointer's contents were accessed. Requiring that as long as the smart pointer exists the memory it manages must contain a valid data value simplifies many things and makes a common kind of error impossible.

Once we have an initialized the `Box`, we can mostly treat it as if it was a normal borrow of the contained data. We can move the data back out onto the stack by dereferencing it:

```
let x = *jack;
```

This moves the `Person` value from inside the `Box` named `jack` to the `x` variable, and renders `jack` unusable.

We can also access the contained data value's data and functions through the `Box`, again as if it were a borrow of the contained data:

```
let x = &jack.name;
println!("The person in the box is {}", x);
```

Here, we're asking to borrow `jack.name` into `x`, then printing out that name. We could have also gotten the same result by doing the following:

```
println!("The person in the box is {}", jack.name);
```

But that actually works in a very different way. The first example borrows the name, and then prints out that borrowed `String` value. The second one actually calls a function called `jack.name.fmt`, which has an immutable borrow as its `self` parameter. This works out because Rust is smart about dereferencing and function calls.

 Where did `fmt` get called? The answer is that `println!` is a *macro*, which means that it's not actually a function, but instead is kind of like pasting some code right into the program here. The pasted code calls `fmt`, so it's as if we called `fmt` ourselves. In Rust, we can recognize macros because their names always end with `!`, and function names never do.

Box and variable size

We've previously bumped into the need for Rust to know exactly how many bytes a particular data value can occupy. Most of the time, Rust can figure that out, and most of the time, it's not a problem, but there are a few cases where it's impossible to define a fixed size for a data value.

One fundamental example is a data structure, such as the following one, where an instance contains other instances of itself:

```
pub struct TreeNode {
    pub value: i32,
    pub left: TreeNode,
    pub right: TreeNode,
}
```

That looks reasonable at first glance, but Rust quite rightly points out that the calculated size is infinite (because the size of a TreeNode is the size of two TreeNodes plus 32 bits):

```
error[E0072]: recursive type `boxes::TreeNode` has infinite size
 --> src/boxes.rs:6:1
  |
6 | pub struct TreeNode {
  | ^^^^^^^^^^^^^^^^^^^ recursive type has infinite size
7 |     pub value: i32,
8 |     pub left: TreeNode,
  |     ------------------ recursive without indirection
9 |     pub right: TreeNode,
  |     ------------------- recursive without indirection
  |
  = help: insert indirection (e.g., a `Box`, `Rc`, or `&`) at some point to make `boxes::TreeNode` representable
```

Just as the compiler suggests, we can fix this with a Box:

```
pub struct TreeNode {
    pub value: i32,
    pub left: Box<TreeNode>,
    pub right: Box<TreeNode>,
}
```

Now, the size of a TreeNode is the size of two Boxes plus 32 bits, which is entirely reasonable.

Box and Any

When a variable's type is `Box<dyn Any>`, it acts much like an `&dyn Any`, but gains a new feature. A normal `&dyn Any` has a `downcast_ref` function that we can use to get a reference to the contained value, if we know what type to use to extract it. Now, `&dyn mut Any` adds a `downcast_mut` that we can use to get a mutable reference. When we have a `Box<dyn Any>`, we have access to both of those functions, but we can also call a plain `downcast` function to move the contained value out of the `Any` and into a variable of the correct type. This consumes the `Box` and the `Any`, and gives us back a new `Box` containing the data value with its correct data type.

> Don't forget that we need to have `use std::any::Any;` in our code if we're going to use the `Any` trait.

We can create a boxed `Any` almost the same way we created a boxed `Person`:

```
let jill: Box<dyn Any> = Box::new(Person { name: "Jill".to_string(),
validated: false });
```

The only difference here is that we're telling Rust that we want the `jill` variable to contain a `Box<dyn Any>` instead of letting it decide for itself that the variable contains a `Box<Person>`.

Now, to access the contained `Person`, we can do this:

```
let real_jill = jill.downcast::<Person>().unwrap();
println!("{}", real_jill.name);
```

Like the other downcast functions, we need to specify which concrete data type we're downcasting for. The downcast function returns a `Result`, which contains a `Box<Person>` if it's successful. Once we have a `Box<Person>`, we can do whatever we like with the `Person` value it contains.

> The `unwrap` function we're calling here consumes a `Result` and returns its contained value if it's a success, or terminates the program with an error message if it's a failure. We use `unwrap` to handle a `Result` when we're very sure that it's going to be a success.

Vec and String

When a data value might *change* size, it pretty much has to be stored on the heap. For this reason, the Rust prelude includes the String and Vec types, which are smart pointers specialized for storing text and variable-length arrays, respectively.

String

We've already seen String several times, when we used it to simplify the ownership of text strings. There are other things we can do with it, though, because the text stored in a String can be changed.

Here, we're changing a String several times, as shown in the following code:

```
let mut text = String::new();
text.push('W');
text.push_str("elcome to mutable strings");
text.insert_str(11, "exciting ");
text.replace_range(28.., "text");
println!("{}", text);
```

Let's take a look at that step by step:

1. On the first line, we're creating an empty String, and storing it in a mutable variable. It has to be mutable, because we're going to change the stored value.
2. On the second line, we're appending a single character to the String.
3. On the third line, we're appending the whole contents of an &str to the String.
4. On the fourth line, we're inserting the whole contents of an &str at byte offset 11 in the string. Remember that Rust starts counting from zero, so the offset of the W in the string is 0.
5. On the fifth line, we're replacing the characters in a range of offsets with a new sequence of characters. The specific range we're using is 28.., which means the range beginning at 28 and going on to infinity (or the end of the String, whichever comes first).
6. Last, we print out the final result of all our manipulations.

We have to be careful about using byte offsets with `String`, because the `String` type always stores text encoded with the UTF-8 encoding. That means that the number of bytes any single character might use can be as little as one, and as large as four bytes. If we try to use an offset that is in the middle of a character, the program will terminate with an error message. `String` and `&str` have an assortment of functions that let us find valid byte offsets within a `String`, or manipulate it without using offsets at all, such as `find`, `lines`, `split_whitespace`, `contains`, `starts_with`, `ends_with`, `split`, `trim`, and `char_indices`.

Using our `text` variable, the data type of `&text` can be `&String` *or* `&str`. Rust's type inference system makes that decision, based on the data type of the variable where the value will be stored, or the function parameter that it will be assigned to, and so on. That also means that any functions that are implemented for `&str` or that take an `&str` parameter can be used on a `String` as well. For example, `str` has a `lines(&self)` function, so we can call `text.lines()`. Further, we can pass a `String` as the text parameter to the `push_str`, `insert_str`, and `replace_range` functions we saw in this example, just as if it was a real `&str`.

Vec

The `Vec` data type stores a *vector*, which is a word commonly used in programming to indicate a one-dimensional, variable-size array. Like actual arrays, they can store multiple data values, as long as those data values all have the same data type. Like `String`s, `Vec`s can change size, and so they are specialized smart pointers that store their contained values on the heap.

To create an empty `Vec`, we can use `Vec::new()`, like so:

```
let mut vector = Vec::new();
```

Then we can append a data value to it using `push`:

```
vector.push(1.5);
```

Now, so far, we haven't said a word about what type of data the vector can contain, and Rust is perfectly happy because we didn't *need* to. Everything we wrote is consistent with the vector containing one of the floating point primitive data types, so that's what Rust figures it contains.

What happens if we do something that isn't consistent, such as try to store an `&str` in the vector?

```
vector.push("nope");
```

Now Rust can't figure out what data type the vector is supposed to contain, so it refuses to compile:

```
error[E0308]: mismatched types
 --> src/vectors.rs:5:17
  |
5 |      vector.push("nope");
  |                  ^^^^^^ expected floating-point variable, found reference
  |
  = note: expected type `{float}`
             found type `&'static str`

error: aborting due to previous error

For more information about this error, try `rustc --explain E0308`.
error: Could not compile `chapter06`.
```

However, we can do something like this:

```
let x: f64 = 99.9;
vector.push(x);
```

Here, we've got a variable named x that has `f64` for its data type. That's compatible with the "some kind of floating point number" that Rust was able to figure out before, so adding it to the vector doesn't cause any problems. In fact, it tells Rust that our earlier `1.5` should be treated as an `f64` too, and that the vector contains `f64` values, specifically.

We used numbers for that example, but Rust can store any data type in a `Vec`, as long is we follow the rule of only one data type per vector.

Adding an `&str` to our vector of numbers was a problem, but we can create a vector of `&str` without any trouble:

```
let mut second_vector = Vec::new();
second_vector.push("This");
second_vector.push("works");
second_vector.push("fine");
```

We can access elements contained in a vector using the same syntax we would use for an array:

```
    println!("{} {} {}.", second_vector[0], second_vector[1],
second_vector[2]);
```

`Vec` implements a number of functions for accessing the stored data values, such as the following:

- `pop`, which removes and returns the last item in the vector
- `remove`, which removes the item at a specific index
- `insert`, which adds an item at a specific index, pushing the item that was at that index and everything after it back one
- `append`, which moves values out of another vector and adds them at the end
- `len`, which just tells us how many items are in the vector
- `iter`, which returns an iterator for the contained data

Creating an empty vector and then pushing a bunch of values to it can get a little bit tedious, so there's a macro to make things easier:

```
    let third_vector = vec!["This", "works", "too"];
```

We recognize the macro by its ! as always, but this time it's not really pretending to be a function. Instead, it almost looks like a prefixed array expression. Macros have a lot of flexibility about how they look, and for this one, looking similar to an array expression makes sense. The end result of this is just like we'd created a vector with `new` and then added information to it with `push`. It's just a more convenient way of writing the same thing.

Rc

There are times when Rust's insistence that each data value has only one owner just doesn't fit our program's data model. What if we're writing a word processing engine, and we wanted people to be able to include the same image in multiple places without wasting memory on duplicates; or what if we were modeling an organization where one person might be referenced by multiple roles?

We could have one definitive owner of the shared information, and use borrows everywhere else, and if that works, it's probably the way to go. There are two situations where it doesn't work, though:

- We don't know how long the lifetimes of each of the users of the shared data value will be
- We need write access to the shared data in at least one of the users

A word processing engine is a good example of problem number one: An image may be used more than once in the same document, but we never know when the user might decide to delete one of them, nor do we know which one will be deleted. Maybe all of them will be deleted, and who knows what order that will happen in or what the timing will be like.

To fully address problem number two, we'll need both the Rc and RefCell data types, so we'll talk about that later in this chapter.

When we find ourselves in a situation where we need to share information without knowing about the relative lifetimes of the various borrows of that information, we can use the Rc smart pointer to make everything work. Rc stands for "reference counted," and what it does is keep track of how many copies of itself exist. When that number reaches zero, the lifetime of the contained data value ends.

Let's look at creating some reference-counted smart pointers:

```
pub fn make_vector_of_rcs() -> Vec<Rc<String>> {
    let ada = Rc::new("Ada".to_string());
    let mel = Rc::new("Mel".to_string());

    return vec![
        Rc::clone(&ada),
        Rc::clone(&mel),
        Rc::clone(&ada),
        Rc::clone(&ada),
        Rc::clone(&mel),
        Rc::clone(&ada),
        Rc::clone(&mel),
    ];
}
```

We created the first Rc values using Rc::new, on the first two lines of the function body. Both of them contain a String value.

After that, we used `Rc::clone` to create several duplicates of each `Rc`. Keep in mind that the `String` values are *not* being duplicated, just the `Rc` smart pointer. The returned vector contains four `Rc`s that share access to the same `ada` string, and three that share access to the same `mel` string.

Then the function's scope ends, and so does the lifetime of the original `ada` and `mel` reference-counted smart pointers. However, the various copies are part of the return value, so their lifetimes do not end, and as a consequence the reference counts of the two string values are still greater than zero, and their lifetimes also do not end.

We used `Rc::clone` here, but if we'd written `ada.clone()` or `mel.clone()`, it would have produced the same result. People usually prefer to write it as `Rc::clone` to make it plain that we're cloning the `Rc`, and not the data value the `Rc` contains.

Now we'll write a short program that relies on user input to determine when the lifetime of each of the `Rc` copies ends. There's no fixed order in which the `Rc`s are to be removed, so the compiler can't know ahead of time when it's safe to clean up their shared data values, but thanks to the reference counting mechanism, the `String` values are retained as long as they are needed, and then their lifetime ends.

Here, we remove elements from the vector based on the user input:

```
let mut ada_and_mel = make_vector_of_rcs();

while ada_and_mel.len() > 0 {
  println!("{:?}", ada_and_mel);

  print!("Remove which: ");
  io::stdout().flush().unwrap();

  let mut line = String::new();
  io::stdin().read_line(&mut line).unwrap();

  let idx: usize = line.trim().parse().unwrap();
  ada_and_mel.remove(idx);
}
```

First, we call our `make_vector_of_rcs` function to create the initial vector of reference-counted smart pointers to the shared data.

Then, we loop as long as there are any values still stored in the vector. Within the loop, we first print out the current vector (the `{:?}` code tells Rust to print out the `'debug'` representation of the vector, which looks like a Rust array expression). Then we print out a prompt, and flush the output stream to make sure the prompt is actually displayed. Then we read a line from the input stream, parse it into an integer, and use that integer as an index to remove an element from the vector.

When we run that program, it looks like this:

```
["Ada", "Mel", "Ada", "Ada", "Mel", "Ada", "Mel"]
Remove which: 3
["Ada", "Mel", "Ada", "Mel", "Ada", "Mel"]
Remove which: 5
["Ada", "Mel", "Ada", "Mel", "Ada"]
Remove which: 2
["Ada", "Mel", "Mel", "Ada"]
Remove which: 3
["Ada", "Mel", "Mel"]
Remove which: 2
["Ada", "Mel"]
Remove which: 1
["Ada"]
Remove which: 0
```

When the last `Rc` that references the "Mel" value is removed, the lifetime of that `String` finally ends, and the same goes for the `String` containing "Ada".

We used `unwrap` a lot in that code, and really, we overused it. Unwrapping the results of `flush` and `read_line` makes sense; if those return a failed `Result`, the program should probably terminate because something has gone wrong on the operating system level. However, unwrapping the result of `parse` is not such a good idea, because a failed result there just means that the user entered something unexpected. We really should have used `match` to respond by printing out a message when the input doesn't parse properly. We also should have checked that the number was the index of a value that was actually within the vector, and not off beyond one of the ends. Rust won't let us access an invalid index, but trying to do so will terminate the program with an error message, which isn't great.

Parsing means taking information encoded as a text string, and turning it into a data value we can actually work with; for example, turning "5" into the number 5. The `parse` function is pretty wild, because it figures out what kind of information we want based on the data type of the variable we're assigning its return value to, and then figures out which function to use to turn a string into that kind of data value. Of course, it can't write that function for us, so it only works for data types that have such a function in the first place. Also, it's really the Rust compiler doing all of the figuring out. The `parse` function just takes advantage of the compiler's rules and inference system.

Weak references

Reference counting has one fatal flaw, which is the reason why it's not used by default for all variables in every programming language: cycles. If two or more reference counted values somehow refer to each other, their lifetimes would never end. They form what is called a *cycle*.

It isn't always obvious when a cycle happens. If A refers to B, which refers to C, which refers to D, which refers to A, we still have a cycle.

We can break cycles by using *weak references*, which are an ancillary data type for `Rc`. When we have an `Rc`, we can call its `downgrade` function (for example, `let weak_mel = Rc::downgrade(&mel)`) to retrieve a `Weak` data value.

We can't actually do anything with a `Weak` except retrieve an `Rc` by calling its `upgrade` function (for example `weak_mel.upgrade()`), but using a `Weak` lets us keep track of a reference-counted value without actually referencing it, which means we can avoid creating cycles while still organizing our information in the way that seems natural.

If the number of `Rc`s that reference a data value is zero, that data value's lifetime ends, *even if there are still `Weak`s that reference the value.*

Because the referenced value might not exist anymore, the `upgrade` function returns an `Option`. When we call `upgrade`, we'll either get a `Some` containing our `Rc`, or we'll get `None`.

So, the pattern here is that we use `Rc` when we want to make sure that the data value sticks around as long as we need it, and `Weak` when we *know* it's going to stick around (for example, when it's referring to the parent node in a tree structure) or when we *don't care* whether it sticks around (for example, when it's a cached value that we can regenerate if it's missing).

Cell and RefCell

Rust's rule that only one block of code can have write access to a data value at any one time is a good one, but sometimes the restrictions that are needed to be sure *when the compiler is running* that this rule will always be followed are too tight. Sometimes, we need the extra freedom that comes from having the rule checked *while the program is running*, instead.

The compiler checks would ensure that the program *can't* break the rule, while the runtime checks ensure that the program *doesn't* break the rule, giving us more flexibility at the cost of some overhead.

To support this option, Rust provides us with the `Cell` and `RefCell` data types, which are smart pointers that allow us to change their contents, even if they are not stored in a mutable variable.

Cell

The `Cell` type stores a single data value, which we can move in and out of the `Cell` even if the `Cell` is not marked as mutable. To move a value into the `Cell`, we can use the following:

- `Cell::new`, because the initial value was moved into the cell when the cell is created
- `set`, to move a new value into the cell, and end the lifetime of the value already stored there
- `replace`, to move a new value into the cell, and move the old value into the current scope

To move a value out of the `Cell`, we can use the following:

- `replace`, to move a new value into the cell, and move the old value into the current scope
- `into_inner`, to consume the cell, and return the value it contained

`Cell`s don't support any operations that would allow us to have an empty `Cell`: they always have to contain something, just like the other smart pointer types.

Let's take a look at a cell in action:

```
let cell = Cell::new("Let me out!".to_string());
println!("{}", cell.replace("Don't put me in there.".to_string()));
println!("{}", cell.replace("I didn't do anything.".to_string()));
cell.set("You'll never hold me, copper!".to_string());
println!("{}", cell.into_inner());
```

Notice that the `cell` variable *is not mutable*. Here, we're setting up a cell, using `replace` a couple of times to retrieve the old value from the `cell` at the same time that we set a new one, and then using `set` to set a new value while discarding the old one, and finally using `into_inner` to get rid of the `cell` while extracting its contained value.

The `into_inner` function moves the contained value out of the `cell`, but that doesn't create an empty `cell` because the `cell` no longer exists. If we tried to access it after calling `into_inner`, we'd get an error from the compiler, as shown in the following screenshot:

```
error[E0382]: use of moved value: `cell`
 --> src/cell_and_refcell.rs:9:20
  |
8 |     println!("{}", cell.into_inner());
  |                    ---- value moved here
9 |     println!("{}", cell.replace("I still didn't do anything.".to_string()));
  |                    ^^^^ value used here after move
  |
  = note: move occurs because `cell` has type `std::cell::Cell<std::string::String>`, which does not implement the `Copy` trait
```

There's one more function that we can use to access the data value contained in a `Cell`, but only if the contained data type has the `Copy` trait: `get`. We could do something like `println!("{}", cell.get())` to leave the content of the `cell` in place while retrieving a copy of it, but only if copying the data value is actually possible.

What's the point?

Okay, so what's this actually good for? We could have just used a mutable variable, and produced the same result with less overhead. Cell (and RefCell) are mostly for use with Rc and similar data types. The Rc type follows Rust's normal rules about mutability, and since it's meant to be a mechanism for accessing a shared data value in many places, that means that the shared value must be immutable.

Unless that value is a Cell or RefCell containing the *real* shared value.

The Cell or RefCell ensures that only one block of code at a time *actually* modifies the shared value, but any of the blocks that have access to it through a clone of the Rc have the *ability* to do so.

RefCell

Cell's semantics of moving the stored data value in and out of the cell are not always convenient to work with, and for large data values, moving them can be an expensive operation that we don't want to keep repeating over and over without need. RefCell to the rescue!

The RefCell type supports RefCell::new, replace, and into_inner, just as Cell does, but it also has functions that allow us to borrow the contained value, either mutably or immutably.

Let's give RefCell a whirl:

```
let refcell = RefCell::new("It's a string".to_string());

match refcell.try_borrow() {
Ok(x) => { println!("Borrowed: {}", x); }
Err(_) => { println!("Couldn't borrow first try"); }
};

let borrowed_mutably = refcell.try_borrow_mut()?;

match refcell.try_borrow() {
Ok(x) => { println!("Borrowed: {}", x); }
Err(_) => { println!("Couldn't borrow second try"); }
};

println!("Mutable borrow is still alive: {}", borrowed_mutably);
```

First, we created a new RefCell, containing a text string. After that, we used the try_borrow function to retrieve an immutable borrow of the contained data value. The rules about borrowing are still enforced, meaning we can't borrow a value if it's mutably borrowed, and we can't mutably borrow a value if the value is already borrowed at all, which means that try_borrow might not actually succeed. Therefore, we have to handle the possibility that it fails, which we're doing here by using a match expression.

Next, we retrieve a mutable borrow and store it in a local variable. The previous borrow's lifetime ended at the end of the chosen block in the match expression, so there are no live borrows and we expect the try_borrow_mut to succeed, but we still need to handle the possibility of failure. In this case, we're using ? to handle the returned Result, which will extract the value of a success, or return a failure to the function that called our current function. If the try_borrow_mut succeeds as expected, that leaves the borrowed_mutably variable containing a mutable reference to refcell's contained data value.

Then we again try to borrow the contained data value, immutably. Since immutable borrows are not compatible with mutable borrows, and our mutable borrow is still around, we expect this attempt to fail.

Arc

There's another layer of complexity when it comes to sharing data between multiple code blocks: threads and multithreading. Rc, Cell, and RefCell are all impossible to share between threads, but the ideas they represent would be useful for enabling communication between threads.

There's a direct equivalent of Rc for use with threads: Arc. An Arc is an *atomic reference-counted smart pointer*, which is valid for sharing between threads thanks to that *atomic*, which basically means that even if two threads try to use it at the same time, it's not going to get messed up or confused.

Arc has a different name and works differently inside, but on the surface it's just like Rc. The things we've learned about how to use an Rc apply to an Arc as well.

It's hard to demonstrate the special features of Arc without using Mutex or RwLock as well, so see the next section for some example code.

Mutex and RwLock

`Mutex` and `RwLock` are both similar to `RefCell` in some ways, but not as closely related as `Arc` is to `Rc`.

It's `Mutex`'s job to make sure that only one thread has access to the contained data at a time. Since it guarantees that only one block of code has access at all at any given time, a `Mutex` can safely provide both read and write access without breaking Rust's rules.

In the following example, we have `Mutex` and `Arc` in action, and some very basic multithreading:

```
let counter = Arc::new(Mutex::new(0));

for _ in 0..10 {
 let local_counter = Arc::clone(&counter);
 thread::spawn(move || {
 let wait = time::Duration::new(random::<u64>() % 8, 0);
 thread::sleep(wait);
 let mut shared = local_counter.lock().unwrap();
 *shared += 1;
 });
}

loop {
    {
        let shared = counter.lock().unwrap();
        println!("{} threads have completed", *shared);

        if *shared >= 10 {
            break;
        };
    };
    thread::sleep(time::Duration::new(1, 0));
}
```

The first thing we're doing is creating a new `Arc` containing a `Mutex`, which in turn contains an integer. So, our integer can only be accessed by one thread at a time, but it can be shared among many and its lifetime will not end until all of them are done with it.

Next, we have a `for` loop, which goes through 10 cycles, and launches a thread on each cycle. Notice how we're creating a clone of the `Arc` *before* we call `thread::spawn`. That's because we're using a *closure* to define what the threads should do. A closure is like a function in a lot of ways, but it can borrow or move local variables into its own scope when it's defined. We need to create the `Arc` value that it's going to move into its own scope, before asking it to perform the move.

> This closure is moving local variables into its own scope because we used the `move` keyword when we defined it, and it's moving the `local_counter` variable specifically simply because we referred to it within the closure.

Within each thread's closure, we ask it to wait for a random duration less than 8 seconds, and then add 1 to the counter. In order to add 1 to the counter, we first have to lock the `Mutex`, so that we can be sure no other thread has access. We do that by calling the `Mutex`'s `lock()` function via the `Arc` (because an `Arc` can pretend to be a normal borrow of the thing inside it). The value that the `lock` function returns both provides us with access to the contained data when we dereference it, and keeps track of how long the `Mutex` should remain locked. When the lifetime of that returned value ends, the `Mutex` is unlocked so that other threads can access the contained data value. If another thread tries to lock the value while it's still locked, `Mutex` makes that other thread wait until it's unlocked before continuing.

> The `lock` function actually returns a `Result`, but we're just unwrapping that here. If the call to `lock` fails, it's because one of the other threads had a bad error while it had the `Mutex` locked, and ending the program is probably the smart thing to do.

Finally, we can just do a `*shared +=1` to actually add 1 to the shared counter.

After that, we have a loop, which locks the `Mutex`, then prints out the current value of the counter, and ends the loop (using the `break` keyword) if it is greater than or equal to 10. If the loop hasn't ended, it then waits one second and does it again.

Notice that within that loop, we have another block expression, and that the `thread::sleep` call is outside of it. That's because of the way `Mutex` works: as long as the returned value's lifetime hasn't ended, the `Mutex` remains locked. We don't want the `Mutex` to be locked while this code is sleeping, so we put the return value into a shorter scope, so that its lifetime would end before we called `thread::sleep`, and the `Mutex` would be unlocked.

An `RwLock` is similar to a `Mutex`, but it has different rules about how access to the contained data value is managed. Instead of a single lock function, `RwLock` has two: `read` and `write`. Any number of threads can call `read` to access the contained information at the same time, but only one thread can use `write` to access it at any given moment, and while a thread has write access, no other threads are allowed to read it. If a thread tries to read or write at a time when it's not allowed, `RwLock` makes the thread wait until what it wants to do is allowed again.

> We don't need to use `read` and `write` together to have both kinds of access. Using `write` implies that we have read access as well.

Summary

In this chapter, we've learned about the following:

- The differences between heap and stack memory
- How to use `Box` to simply store something on the heap, when we wish to do so
- How to use `Rc` to manage the lifetime of a data value that is needed in many scopes with varying lifetimes
- How to use `Cell` and `RefCell` to allow write access to data stored in an `Rc`
- How to use `Arc`, `Mutex`, and `RwLock` to manage sharing information between threads

In the next chapter, we're going to be looking at generic types, and how to use generic type parameters for our own data types.

7
Generic Types

Sometimes, the details of a data type just don't matter. Our code would work just as well no matter what the data type is, as long as it's *something*.

We've seen examples of this sort of situation many times already, such as with `Result`, `Option`, `Rc`, and so on. All of them, and many more, can work with a wide range of different data types, because they have one or more *generic type parameters*.

In this chapter, we're going to do the following:

- Learn what generic type parameters are
- Learn how to apply generic type parameters to data types
- Learn how to apply generic type parameters to functions
- Learn how generic types and trait objects differ
- Create a complete and useful binary tree data structure

Types with generic type parameters

When a data type has generic type parameters, it's not, strictly speaking, actually a data type at all. It is a whole family of data types. Let's look at `Option` for a moment. `Option` is defined as follows:

```
pub enum Option<T> {
    None,
    Some(T),
}
```

This means that it has one generic type parameter with the name T. If we try to use Option without specifying a type for that generic type parameter, Rust will report an error:

```
let x: Option = None;
```

It produces this error:

```
error[E0243]: wrong number of type arguments: expected 1, found 0
 --> src/main.rs:2:12
  |
2 |     let x: Option = None;
  |            ^^^^^^ expected 1 type argument
```

What that's telling us, in essence, is that Option isn't a usable data type. However, Option<u32> is, as is Option<String>, Option<Result<f64, String>>, and so on. Moreover, Option<u32> and Option<String> are not the same type, and Rust won't pretend that they are. They're two different data types that have the same shape, as it were.

When we write Option<String>, we're telling Rust that it should make a data type by substituting String for the T in the definition of Option.

Limiting what types can be used for type parameters

Sometimes, we need our type to have generic type parameters, but we don't want them to be *totally* generic. For example, we might need the type that's substituted for the parameter to be able to be moved between threads, or to support transformation into String, or any number of other things. Fortunately, Rust provides a way for us to do that.

We limit the domain of a generic type parameter by requiring it to have one or more traits. This is called a trait bound. Let's look at a basic binary tree data structure as an example.

 A binary tree is made up of nodes. Each node has a key, an associated value, and two sub-trees: one for nodes with keys that are less than the current node's key, and one for nodes with keys that are greater. Finding a node with a particular key in the tree is just a matter of comparing it to the root node's key, then if it isn't the same, picking either the lesser or greater tree, and doing the same thing there, and so on.

Here are a pair of structures that represent a binary tree, with generic type parameters for the key and value types, and a trait bound on the key type to make sure it actually supports the comparisons we need for a binary tree key:

```
struct TreeNode<K, V> where K: PartialOrd + PartialEq {
    key: K,
    value: V,
    lesser: Option<Box<TreeNode<K, V>>>,
    greater: Option<Box<TreeNode<K, V>>>,
}
```

Here is the second structure, which gives us a way to store an empty tree:

```
pub struct Tree<K, V> where K: PartialOrd + PartialEq {
    root: Option<Box<TreeNode<K, V>>>,
}
```

We need the second structure so that a tree containing no data can be represented. On both of these structures, we've placed the names of the generic type parameters between < and > after the structure name, but then we included a where clause that says that K: PartialOrd + PartialEq. That means that any data type that is substituted for K *must* implement both the PartialOrd trait and the PartialEq trait. If we try to use a data type that does not implement both traits, the compiler will reject it.

 We'll examine the specific meanings of PartialOrd and PartialEq in Chapter 8, *Important Standard Traits*. Roughly, they mean that the concepts of *greater* and *lesser* apply to the key.

We've also specified that lesser and greater in TreeNode and root in Tree are variables with the Option<Box<TreeNode<K, V>>> data type . That means that they are optional (they can contain a meaningful value, or None), and if they contain a meaningful value, it is stored on the heap, and that value stored on the heap is a TreeNode with K as the data type of its key, and V as the data type of its value.

Implementing functionality for types with generic type parameters

If we want to have functions that are part of a type with generic type parameters, we need to have an implementation block, the same as if the type didn't have those parameters, but we need to parameterize the implementation block, too.

Here is the beginning of our implementation block for the `TreeNode` type:

```
impl<K, V> TreeNode<K, V> where K: PartialOrd + PartialEq {
```

Now, `TreeNode<K, V>` is the data type we're implementing functionality for. It's the `impl<K, V>` part that tells the compiler that K and V are generic type parameters, and it's `K: PartialOrd + PartialEq` that tells it the trait bounds for those parameters. It does not just use the same generic type parameters and trait bounds that were specified for the data type, because implementation blocks are allowed to differ from the data type; for example, there's an implementation block for `Box<Any>` that provides the `downcast` function for a boxed `Any`, which is not a part of `Box` under other circumstances. If the implementation block's trait bounds match what is actually being using for type parameters, the functions in the block are available. If they do not, the functions are not available.

Inside the implementation block, we can use K and V as the names of data types:

```
fn set(&mut self, key: K, value: V) {
    if key == self.key {
        self.value = value;
    }
    else if key < self.key {
        match self.lesser {
            None => {
                self.lesser = Some(
                    Box::new(TreeNode {key, value, lesser: None,
                    greater: None })
                );
            },
            Some(ref mut lesser) => {
                lesser.set(key, value);
            }
        }
    }
    else {
        match self.greater {
            None => {
                self.greater = Some(
                    Box::new(TreeNode {key, value, lesser: None,
                    greater: None })
                );
            }
            Some(ref mut greater) => {
                greater.set(key, value);
            }
        }
    }
```

```
            }
    }
```

Here we have the code to associate a key with a value inside our binary tree. It starts off with a pretty standard function definition, except that we're using K and V to specify the data types of the key and value parameters. We mutably borrow self because setting a contained value is a mutation.

Inside the function, we first compare the current node's key to the key we're looking for, and if they're the same, we just assign the value to the current node.

Next, we check whether the key we're looking for is less than or greater than the current node's key, and use that to select which branch of the tree to travel down. Either way, we use a match expression to figure out whether there actually is a branch on that side, and if there's not, we create one containing the specified key and value. If there *is* a branch on that side, we call that node's set function, which does the same thing all over again except with a different self.

Using generic types as function return values

Within an implementation block that has generic type parameters, we can use those parameter names as part of function return values, too.

Here is an example function that uses generic type parameter names in its return data type:

```
fn get_ref(&self, key: K) -> Result<&V, String> {
    if key == self.key {
        return Ok(&self.value);
    }
    else if key < self.key {
        match self.lesser {
            None => {
                return Err("No such key".to_string());
            }
            Some(ref lesser) => {
                return lesser.get_ref(key);
            }
        }
    }
    else {
        match self.greater {
```

```
                    None => {
                        return Err("No such key".to_string());
                    }
                    Some(ref greater) => {
                        return greater.get_ref(key);
                    }
                }
            }
        }
    }
```

This function looks up a key in the binary tree, and returns an immutable borrow of the associated value, or an error message if the key is not present in the tree.

It's structured very similarly to the `set` function we saw before, but since we're not changing anything or asking for a mutable borrow, `self` can be a plain old immutable borrow as well.

Compiler errors involving generic type parameters

Our tree structure requires that the data type used for the key has to have the `PartialOrd` and `PartialEq` traits. The `&str` type happens to have those traits, so we can use an `&str` for the key:

```
let mut tree: Tree<&'static str, f32> = Tree::new();

tree.set("first key", 12.65);
tree.set("second key", 99.999);
tree.set("third key", -128.5);
tree.set("fourth key", 67.21);

println!("tree.get_ref(\"third key\") is {}", match tree.get_ref("third
key") {
    Err(_) => {println!("Invalid!"); &0.0},
    Ok(x) => x,
});
```

Here, we've created a `Tree<&'static str, f32>`, or a tree that maps static strings to 32-bit floating point numbers. If we compile and run a complete program containing that snippet, everything works beautifully.

This data type, on the other hand, does not have the `PartialOrd` trait:

```
pub enum NotOrdered {
    A,
    B,
    C,
}
```

If we substitute `NotOrdered` for `&'static str` as the key type for the tree, we suddenly get seven different compiler errors, which probably fill up the entire screen. Most of them look something like this:

```
error[E0599]: no method named `get_ref` found for type `Tree<NotOrdered, f32>` in the current scope
  --> src/main.rs:145:62
   |
88 |   pub struct Tree<K, V> where K: PartialOrd + PartialEq {
   |   ----------------------------------------------------- method `get_ref` not found for this
...
145 |       println!("tree.get_ref(\"third key\") is {}", match tree.get_ref("third key") {
   |                                                                  ^^^^^^^
   |
   = note: the method `get_ref` exists but the following trait bounds were not satisfied:
           `NotOrdered : std::cmp::PartialOrd`
           `NotOrdered : std::cmp::PartialEq`
```

This is telling us that the function was defined inside an implementation block that requires `PartialOrd` and `PartialEq`. Since our `NotOrdered` data type doesn't have those traits, the function we're trying to call doesn't exist, and the compiler is telling us that.

Up at the top of the list of errors, and possibly scrolled right off the screen, is a different error message:

```
error[E0277]: can't compare `NotOrdered` with `NotOrdered`
  --> src/main.rs:138:19
   |
138 |       let mut tree: Tree<NotOrdered, f32> = Tree::new();
   |                     ^^^^^^^^^^^^^^^^^^^^^^ no implementation for `NotOrdered < NotOrdered` and `NotOrdered > NotOrdered`
   |
   = help: the trait `std::cmp::PartialOrd` is not implemented for `NotOrdered`
note: required by `Tree`
  --> src/main.rs:88:1
   |
88 |   pub struct Tree<K, V> where K: PartialOrd + PartialEq {
   |   ^^^^^^^^^^^^^^^^^^^^^^^^^^^^^^^^^^^^^^^^^^^^^^^^^^^^^^
```

This error message is somewhat more helpful than the other one, but it stems from the same cause. Our `Tree` data type requires a key type whose values can be compared to other values of the same type, and `NotOrdered` just doesn't provide that.

Generic types on functions outside of implementation blocks

It's possible to use generic type parameters for functions even when they're not part of an implementation block. That looks like this:

```
fn print_generic<T>(value: T) where T: Display {
    println!("{}", value);
}
```

This function has a generic type parameter, T, which can be any data type that has the Display trait. That means that, if this function is defined, we can do things like this:

```
print_generic(12.7);
print_generic("Hello");
print_generic(75);
```

Each of those lines calls a different print_generic function, specialized for the data type of the parameter. The compiler generates code for each version of print_generic that we use, each one accepting a different data type for its parameter.

 Of course, print_generic doesn't do anything that the plain println! macro doesn't, but it serves to demonstrate the ways of generic type parameters for standalone functions.

Alternative ways to write trait bounds

So far, we've been writing trait bounds as a where clause, but there are two alternative ways of writing them. The where clause is nice because it's somewhat out of the way, allowing us to write even complex trait bounds without interfering with reading the rest of the function or data type declaration.

The first alternative is to put the trait bounds alongside the generic type parameter names, like this:

```
impl<K: PartialOrd + PartialEq, V> TreeNode<K, V> {
```

For a standalone function, that technique looks like this:

```
fn print_generic<T: Display>(value: T) {
```

This can be good for data types or functions that only have simple trait bounds, but we can see that even with just two required traits, the `TreeNode` implementation block is getting a little hard to read. The trait bound kind of breaks up the flow and makes us go looking for the data type's name when we want to find it.

There's another way of specifying trait bounds that only works for functions:

```
fn requires_trait(value: impl Display)   {
```

What we're saying here is that the `value` parameter can be any data type that has the `Display` trait. As with any other function with generic type parameters, the compiler will generate a different version of the function for each data type that is actually used for `value`. However, using this syntax, we didn't give the generic type parameter a name, so we can't refer to it elsewhere in the function.

Within the body of the function, that's not usually much of a problem, because we can usually skip specifying data types inside the function body and just rely on the compiler to figure it out.

We can also use a similar syntax to specify the return type of our function, which is handy because if we don't have a name for one or more of the parameter types, it can be hard to write the return type:

```
fn requires_trait(value: impl Display) -> impl Display {
```

This doesn't mean that the function could return any data type as long as it implements `Display` (the correct way to do that would be to return a trait object, such as `Box<dyn Display>`), but all we care about is that the return type *does* implement `Display`, and we want the compiler to figure out the details of the return type beyond that.

To make that clear, here is a function that tries to return two different data types, both of which implement `Display`:

```
fn faulty_return(sel: bool) -> impl Display {
    if sel {
        return 52;
    } else {
        return "Oh no";
    }
}
```

Here is the error message that Rust gives when we try to compile it:

```
error[E0308]: mismatched types
   --> src/main.rs:155:16
    |
155 |             return "Oh no";
    |                    ^^^^^^^ expected integral variable, found reference
    |
    = note: expected type `{integer}`
               found type `&'static str`
```

When it finds the `return 52`, Rust checks that `52` implements `Display` (it does) and decides that the actual return type of the function is some form of integer. Then, it finds the second `return` and decides that something is wrong, because even though "Oh no" also implements `Display`, it's definitely not an integer. Returning an `impl Display` or similar doesn't mean returning anything that implements `Display`; it means figuring out the specific type we're returning, as long as it implements `Display`.

Generic types versus trait objects

We can use trait objects in a very similar way to generic type parameters. From one point of view, these two functions do the same thing:

```
fn print_generic<T>(value: T) where T: Display {
    println!("{}", value);
}
```

This might seem like it does the same thing as the previous code:

```
fn print_trait(value: &dyn Display) {
    println!("{}", value);
}
```

The first has a generic type parameter with a trait bound, the second accepts a trait object, which means both of them can work with many different data types, as long as the type in question has the `Display` trait.

Underneath, though, they're very different. The generic function is used to generate a version of the function that is specialized for each data type that is passed to it, while the compiler is running. That means that when we call the function while the program is running,the computer doesn't have to spend any time at all considering the differences between various data types. It just calls the function the compiler told it to use, which is the version specialized for the data type that's actually being used. This is faster, but all the various versions of generic functions make the program a little larger.

 This process of turning a generic type-based pattern for a function into multiple actual functions specialized for specific types is called *monomorphization*.

The function that accepts a trait object as its parameter, on the other hand, has only one version, but the computer has to deal with the differences between the various data types that have the `Display` trait while it's running. This is slower, but requires a little less memory.

As a rule of thumb, opt to use generic type parameters when you can. We do things at runtime when they can't be done at compile time.

Higher-order functions and trait bounds that represent functions

A higher-order function is a function that takes another function, or a closure, as a parameter. In Rust, there are three somewhat unusual traits that allow us to specify a function or closure as a parameter's trait bound: `Fn`, `FnOnce`, and `FnMut`.

The differences between these traits are defined by what kind of variable access they permit:

- `FnOnce` is the most widely applicable of these traits, because it has the fewest requirements on what types can implement it. An `FnOnce` only guarantees that it is safe to call it once. A function that consumes `self` is an example of a natural `FnOnce`, because having consumed `self`, it no longer has a `self` to be called on in future. Functions and closures that are safe to be called more than once still implement `FnOnce`, because calling them exactly once isn't an error. That means that a variable that is constrained to be an `FnOnce` can accept any sort of function or closure.

- `FnMut` is the next most widely applicable trait. An `FnMut` guarantees that it is safe to call it more than once, but it doesn't promise not to change variable values elsewhere in the code via mutable borrows. A function that uses `&mut self` is an example of a natural `FnMut`, because it might change one or more of the variables contained in its `self`. Functions and closures that can't or don't actually change any outside variables still implement `FnMut`, because using them in a place where mutating is allowed isn't an error.
- `Fn` is the least applicable, since it guarantees that it can be called multiple times and it will not change any outside variables. Anything that is `Fn` can safely be used where an `FnMut` or `FnOnce` was expected, but the reverse is not true.

That means that when we're the receiver, we should prefer to accept `FnOnce` if possible, or `FnMut` as a second choice, and `Fn` as the last choice when we truly need all of those guarantees, so as to give the people who are sending the data value to us the maximum flexibility in what they choose to send.

Here is a very simple higher-order function, which uses a trait bound to specify what kind of function can be assigned to the `f` parameter:

```
fn higher_order(f: impl FnOnce(u32) -> u32) {
    f(5);
}
```

So, that looks a little odd. `FnOnce(u32) -> u32` is the complete name of the trait that we're requiring data types for `f` to implement. The special syntax that allows us to specify the parameter and return types for `Fn`, `FnMut`, and `FnOnce` is unique to those traits; we can't do similar things anywhere else.

Just to be clear, that function definition could have also been written as follows:

```
fn higher_order2<F>(f: F) where F: FnOnce(u32) -> u32 {
    f(5);
}
```

We could also have written the same thing as follows:

```
fn higher_order3<F: FnOnce(u32) -> u32>(f: F) {
    f(5);
}
```

All of the preceding code means the same thing: the function's `f` parameter needs to implement the `FnOnce` trait, and accept a single `u32` parameter, and return a `u32`.

Here's a bit of code that calls our `higher_order` function and passes it a closure to be used as the value of `f`:

```
let mut y = "y".to_string();
higher_order(|x: u32| {
    y.push('X');
    println!("In the closure, y is now {}", y);
    x
});
println!("After higher_order, y is {}", y);
```

This closure has one parameter named `x`, defined between the | and | symbols, but it also accesses the `y` variable that was defined on the first line. In addition, it changes the value of that variable, meaning it requires mutable access. Thus, this closure implements `FnOnce` and `FnMut`, but not `Fn`.

If we change `higher_order` to require the `Fn` trait and try compiling this code, we get a compiler error, as shown in the following screenshot:

```
error[E0387]: cannot borrow data mutably in a captured outer variable in an `Fn` closure
  --> src/main.rs:185:9
    |
185 |             y.push('X');
    |             ^

help: consider changing this closure to take self by mutable reference
  --> src/main.rs:184:18
    |
184 |           higher_order(|x: u32| {
    |                        ^
185 | |             y.push('X');
186 | |             println!("In the closure, y is now {}", y);
187 | |             x
188 | |         });
    | |_____^
```

This error is not particularly illuminating. What it means is that we told `higher_order` to require an `Fn`, and then we passed it a closure that therefore *must* be an `Fn`, but we tried to perform a mutating operation inside of the closure, where we don't have a mutable `borrow` because Rust is sure that the closure must have the `Fn` trait, so it reports an error about trying a mutating operation on a non-mutable variable.

All we need to do to fix this is change the trait bound on the `higher_order` function's `f` parameter back to `FnOnce` (or `FnMut`) so that the closure is allowed to perform the `push` operation on `y`.

Once we restore f to have the proper trait bound, what does this code actually do?:

1. Creates a mutable variable y containing a String
2. Constructs a closure that captures a mutable borrow of the y variable, and accepts an x parameter
3. Passes that closure to higher_order as the value of the f parameter
4. higher_order then calls f (which is our closure), passing it 5 as the value of its x parameter
5. Within the closure, the following occurs:
    1. The character 'X' is appended to the string stored in y
    2. The new value of y is printed
    3. The value of x is returned, and becomes the result of the f(5) expression
6. higher_order returns
7. The current value of the y variable is printed

 Notice that the code inside the closure does not run until the closure is called, but it has access to the variables that were defined in the scope where it was created.

Both of the printouts of y print the string yX, because they are both referring to the same actual variable, whether directly or via a mutable borrow.

Complete implementation of a binary tree with generic type parameters

We've finally progressed far enough in our journey through Rust that we can produce something truly useful. Our binary tree could still be improved in any number of ways, but it does what it was designed to do: it allows us to easily store and retrieve any number of key/value pairs.

We made no effort to ensure that the binary tree remains balanced, meaning that the left and right branches of each node are approximately the same height, because that wouldn't have added anything to our discussion of generic types. If we had, this data structure would also be guaranteed to be efficient. Balanced binary trees are close to being as good as you can get when it comes to arbitrary key/value data structures.

So, here we have a complete, useful data structure. First we have the actual structure that stores the tree node data:

```
struct TreeNode<K, V> where K: PartialOrd + PartialEq {
    key: K,
    value: V,
    lesser: Option<Box<TreeNode<K, V>>>,
    greater: Option<Box<TreeNode<K, V>>>,
}
```

Next, we have the implementation block to define the functionality of the `TreeNode` type, starting with the `set` function, which associates a key with a value:

```
impl<K, V> TreeNode<K, V> where K: PartialOrd + PartialEq {
    fn set(&mut self, key: K, value: V) {
        if key == self.key {
            self.value = value;
        }
        else if key < self.key {
            match self.lesser {
                None => {
                    self.lesser = Some(Box::new(TreeNode {key, value,
                        lesser: None, greater: None }));
                },
                Some(ref mut lesser) => {
                    lesser.set(key, value);
                }
            }
        }
        else {
            match self.greater {
                None => {
                    self.greater = Some(Box::new(TreeNode {key, value,
                        lesser: None, greater: None }));
                }
                Some(ref mut greater) => {
                    greater.set(key, value);
                }
            }
        }
```

```
        }
    }
```

The `get_ref` and `get_mut` functions are structured very similarly to the `set` function, because all three of them use the same mechanism to search the tree for a node with the correct key:

```
fn get_ref(&self, key: K) -> Result<&V, String> {
    if key == self.key {
        return Ok(&self.value);
    }
    else if key < self.key {
        match self.lesser {
            None => {
                return Err("No such key".to_string());
            }
            Some(ref lesser) => {
                return lesser.get_ref(key);
            }
        }
    }
    else {
        match self.greater {
            None => {
                return Err("No such key".to_string());
            }
            Some(ref greater) => {
                return greater.get_ref(key);
            }
        }
    }
}

fn get_mut(&mut self, key: K) -> Result<&mut V, String> {
    if key == self.key {
        return Ok(&mut self.value);
    }
    else if key < self.key {
        match self.lesser {
            None => {
                return Err("No such key".to_string());
            }
            Some(ref mut lesser) => {
                return lesser.get_mut(key);
            }
        }
    }
    else {
```

```
            match self.greater {
                None => {
                    return Err("No such key".to_string());
                }
                Some(ref mut greater) => {
                    return greater.get_mut(key);
                }
            }
        }
    }
}
```

Next comes the definition of our `Tree` data type, which provides the public interface to our data structure, and allows us to have an empty tree:

```
pub struct Tree<K, V> where K: PartialOrd + PartialEq {
    root: Option<Box<TreeNode<K, V>>>,
}
```

And now the implementation block for `Tree`, with the public functions that provide us with a way to interact with `TreeNodes`:

```
impl<K, V> Tree<K, V> where K: PartialOrd + PartialEq {
    pub fn new() -> Tree<K, V> {
        Tree { root: None }
    }

    pub fn set(&mut self, key: K, value: V) {
        match self.root {
            None => {
                self.root = Some(Box::new(TreeNode { key, value,
                lesser: None, greater: None }));
            }
            Some(ref mut root) => {
                root.set(key, value);
            }
        }
    }

    pub fn get_ref(&self, key: K) -> Result<&V, String> {
        match self.root {
            None => {
                return Err("No such key".to_string());
            }
            Some(ref root) => {
                return root.get_ref(key);
            }
        }
    }
```

```
        }

        pub fn get_mut(&mut self, key: K) -> Result<&mut V, String> {
            match self.root {
                None => {
                    return Err("No such key".to_string());
                }
                Some(ref mut root) => {
                    return root.get_mut(key);
                }
            }
        }
    }
}
```

Finally, we have a main function to actually use our tree, so we can see it in action:

```
fn main() {
    let mut tree: Tree<&'static str, f32> = Tree::new();

    tree.set("first key", 12.65);
    tree.set("second key", 99.999);
    tree.set("third key", -128.5);
    tree.set("fourth key", 67.21);

    println!("tree.get_ref(\"third key\") is {}", match
     tree.get_ref("third key") {
        Err(_) => {println!("Invalid!"); &0.0},
        Ok(x) => x,
    });
}
```

Summary

In this chapter, we have done the following:

- Looked at generic type parameters for data types and for functions
- Learned how to limit generic type parameters so that we can be sure the concrete types chosen implement the proper traits
- Seen various compiler errors relating to generic types, and what they mean
- Learned how to use trait bounds and the `Fn`, `FnMut`, and `FnOnce` traits to create higher-order functions
- Learned about the differences and similarities between using generic types and using trait objects
- Taken our knowledge from this chapter and previous chapters and built a binary tree data structure

In the next chapter, we're going to conclude our Rust journey by looking at many more traits, learning what they mean and how to implement them.

Summary

In this chapter we have:

-
-
-
-
-
-

8
Important Standard Traits

As we've seen already, traits are an important part of the Rust ecosystem. The traits that are built into the Rust standard library affect many things, including even what operators can be used on a particular data value. In this chapter, we're going to review many of these traits, and see how to implement them on our own data types.

In this chapter, we're going to do the following:

- Look at an assortment of traits defined by the Rust standard library
- Learn about the meanings and implications of those traits
- Learn about what traits are applied automatically
- Learn how to use the `derive` command to generate trait implementations for select traits
- Learn how to manually implement the remaining traits

Traits that can be derived

For some traits, the compiler itself knows how to implement them for a type. If we want them, we only have to tell it that we do, and it will take care of the rest for us.

 We still have the option of manually implementing derivable traits, but that would usually just be a waste of time.

Telling the compiler that we want a data type to have a derivable trait is easy.

Here, we're telling it that we want our `CopyExample` enumeration to implement `Copy` and `Clone`:

```
#[derive(Copy, Clone)]
pub enum CopyExample {
    Good,
    Bad,
}
```

A trait can only be derived if the people who created the trait were able to write a program to generate the trait implementation. When we write `#[derive(Copy, Clone)]`, we're telling the compiler to go find those programs for deriving `Copy` and `Clone` in the source code of the packages where the traits were defined, and run those programs to generate the source code for the trait implementations before it continues compiling. If the decisions that need to be made to implement a trait are too complex for a program to make without user input, the trait can't be derived.

Clone

The `Clone` trait means that it is possible to make an explicit copy of a data value. The compiler won't ever do it automatically, but when we want to copy a value, we can do so by calling its `Clone` function.

Deriving the `Clone` trait looks like this:

```
#[derive(Clone)]
pub enum CloneExample {
    Good,
    Bad,
}
```

Copy

The `Copy` trait means that creating a copy of the data value is just a matter of copying the bits that make up its representation. If the data value contains any borrows or uses heap memory, it can't have the `Copy` trait.

The compiler will automatically copy data values that have the `Copy` trait when it would have otherwise moved them.

Since anything that has the Copy trait can certainly be duplicated on request as well, Copy requires Clone to be implemented.

Deriving Copy looks like this:

```
#[derive(Copy, Clone)]
pub enum CopyExample {
    Good,
    Bad,
}
```

Debug

The Debug trait tells Rust how to format the data value for debugging output. One place this is used is if we use {:?} instead of {} as the substitution marker for the data value in println! or print!.

Since the debugging representation of a data value should be pretty close to the way it would be represented in the source code, Rust is able to derive it for us automatically.

Deriving Debug looks like this:

```
#[derive(Debug)]
pub enum DebugExample {
    Good,
    Bad,
}
```

PartialEq

The PartialEq trait represents the ability to compare the data value with another one to determine whether they are equal. It does *not* imply that a value is considered equal to itself, however.

The PartialEq trait is used by the compiler to implement the == comparison operation.

Floating point numbers are the classic example of a data type that has PartialEq, because the floating point representation of a NaN or Not a Number value is not considered equal to itself.

Deriving `PartialEq` looks like this:

```
#[derive(PartialEq)]
pub enum PartialEqSelf {
    Good,
    Bad,
}
```

However, that derivation only compares two `PartialEqSelf` data values. If we want to enable an equality comparison with data values of other types, we need to implement the trait manually.

Here, we have a manual implementation of the trait, enabling comparison with the `u32` data type:

```
pub enum PartialEqU32 {
    Good,
    Bad,
}

impl PartialEq<u32> for PartialEqU32 {
    fn eq(&self, other: &u32) -> bool {
        match self {
            PartialEqU32::Good => other % 2 == 0,
            PartialEqU32::Bad => other % 2 == 1,
        }
    }
}
```

Here, we've arranged for the `PartialEqU32::Good` value to compare as equal to even number `u32`s, and `PartialEqU32::Bad` to compare equal to odd number `u32`.

Eq

The `Eq` trait means the same thing that `PartialEq` does, *except* that a data value is always equal to itself.

Implementing the `Eq` trait requires implementing the `PartialEq` trait as well, and the only thing it does beyond what `PartialEq` does is provide the compiler with the hint that it doesn't need to bother running the `Eq` function when both sides of the comparison are the same data value.

Deriving `Eq` looks like this:

```
#[derive(Eq, PartialEq)]
pub enum EqExample {
    Good,
    Bad,
}
```

PartialOrd

The `PartialOrd` trait represents the ability to define some sort of ordering between two data values, so we can say one of them is less than the other, or greater than the other, or that they're the same, *or that the ordering relation does not apply to these values*. That last one is the reason why this is a *partial* ordering.

Since *they're the same* is a valid result of the comparison, implementing `PartialOrd` requires the implemention of `PartialEq`.

As with `PartialEq`, we can derive an implementation that compares two data values of the same type, but we can also manually implement the trait to allow comparison with data of different types.

Here, we have the automatic derivation of the trait:

```
#[derive(PartialOrd, PartialEq)]
pub enum PartialOrdSelf {
    Good,
    Bad,
}
```

Here, we have implemented it manually to support comparison with a different data type:

```
pub enum PartialOrdU32 {
 Good,
 Bad,
}

impl PartialEq<u32> for PartialOrdU32 {
    fn eq(&self, _other: &u32) -> bool {
        false
    }
}

impl PartialOrd<u32> for PartialOrdU32 {
    fn partial_cmp(&self, _other: &u32) -> Option<Ordering> {
```

```
            match self {
                PartialOrdU32::Good => Some(Ordering::Greater),
                PartialOrdU32::Bad => None,
            }
        }
    }
```

Here, we're telling Rust that a `PartialOrdU32::Good` value is always greater than any u32 value, but a `PartialOrdU32::Bad` value does not have any relation to any u32 value at all.

Ord

`Ord` is like `PartialOrd`, except that it doesn't allow the option of returning a "no relation" value; for any pair of values, either they are equal, or one is less than the other.

`Ord` is used by the compiler to implement the < (less than), > (greater than), <= (less than or equal), and >= (greater than or equal) comparison operators.

If a data type has the `Ord` trait, it has to also have the `PartialOrd`, `Eq`, and `PartialEq` traits. Like those traits, it can be manually implemented to enable comparisons between different data types, but we have to be very careful that the results returned by the various functions that are used to implement those traits agree with each other. When we derive the traits, we don't have to worry about that.

Here's an example of deriving `Ord`:

```
#[derive(Ord, Eq, PartialOrd, PartialEq)]
pub enum OrdExample {
    Good,
    Bad,
}
```

Hash

The `Hash` trait enables a data value to be used as a key in several of Rust's standard library data structures, such as `HashMap` and `HashSet`.

Deriving the `Hash` trait looks like this:

```
#[derive(Hash)]
pub enum HashExample {
    Good,
    Bad,
}
```

While `Eq` and `PartialEq` are not actually required to implement `Hash`, if they are implemented, they need to agree with it, which is to say that if two values are equal, their hash values should also be equal. The automatically generated implementations have this property, so we only need to worry about it if we're doing manual implementations.

Default

When the `Default` trait is implemented for a type, it makes it possible for us to request a default value for that type of data.

When we derive `Default` for a data type, it sets the default value for that type to be made up of the default values for all of the contained data types, so when we do this:

```
#[derive(Default)]
pub struct DefaultExample {
    name: String,
    value: i32,
}
```

What we're doing is setting the default for the `DefaultExample` type to be a `DefaultExample` containing the default values of a `String` and an `i32`.

We can request a default value like this:

```
let x: DefaultExample = Default::default();
println!("Default String is {:?}, default i32 is {:?}", x.name, x.value);
```

Traits that enable operators

Most of the operators and the special syntax of Rust are backed up by traits, which tell the compiler how to perform the operation on the specific data type it's looking at. We've seen some of those already, but many of them can't be derived, so if we want to enable that syntax for our data types, we need to implement them manually.

Add, Mul, Sub, and Div

The Add, Mul, Sub, and Div traits represent the ability to add, multiply, subtract, or divide two values. These traits are used by the compiler to implement the +, *, -, and / operators.

Notice that if the values of self and other do not have the Copy trait, they are moved into the implementation function and consumed.

All of these traits follow the same pattern, so here's an example implementation of Add:

```
pub enum AddExample {
    One,
    Two,
    Three,
    Many,
}

impl Add for AddExample {
    type Output = AddExample;

    fn add(self, other: AddExample) -> AddExample {
        match (self, other) {
            (AddExample::One, AddExample::One) => AddExample::Two,
            (AddExample::One, AddExample::Two) => AddExample::Three,
            (AddExample::Two, AddExample::One) => AddExample::Three,
            _ => AddExample::Many,
        }
    }
}
```

Mul, Sub, and Div follow the same pattern.

What we've defined here is a very primitive form of counting, that considers any number greater than 3 to be "many".

Inside the impl block, we have type Output = AddExample;. That's a bit of new syntax we haven't seen before. What we're doing is setting the Output *associated type* for this implementation, which is fed back into the trait definition to be used in declaring the signature of the add function. After all, we're returning an AddExample here, and there was no such type when the trait was originally defined. That's not a problem, though, because the trait says that the add function returns a data value of type Output, and we've just told it that Output is an alias for AddExample.

We can also implement adding data of two different types together, by implementing Add<OtherType> for OneType to represent the ability to have a OneType value on the left side of the + and an OtherType value on the right, similarly to the way we were able to create comparisons between two different types earlier in the chapter. The same trick works for Mul, Sub, and Div as well.

AddAssign, MulAssign, SubAssign, and DivAssign

These traits enable the +=, *=, -=, and /= operators for the types that implement them.

They are similar to the Add, Sub, Mul, and Div traits, with the difference that their implementation functions take &mut self instead of plain self. Instead of consuming their left-side input, they have the ability to change its contained value.

All of these traits follow the same pattern, so here's an example implementation of AddAssign:

```
pub enum AddExample {
  One,
  Two,
  Three,
  Many,
}

impl AddAssign for AddExample {
    fn add_assign(&mut self, other: AddExample) {
        *self = match (&self, other) {
            (AddExample::One, AddExample::One) => AddExample::Two,
            (AddExample::One, AddExample::Two) => AddExample::Three,
            (AddExample::Two, AddExample::One) => AddExample::Three,
            _ => AddExample::Many,
        };
    }
}
```

Apart from the differences based on assigning the new value to &mut self, this is much like the implementation of the add function for the Add trait, which isn't very surprising.

In particular, while it doesn't consume its self, it does still consume the value on the right-hand side of the operand, assuming that value doesn't have the Copy trait.

BitAnd

The `BitAnd` trait enables the `&` operator for types that implement it. This operator is used for computing the *bitwise and* value of two integers (hence the name), but has different meanings for various other data types.

Implementing `BitAnd` looks like this:

```
pub enum BitExample {
    Yes,
    No,
}

impl BitAnd for BitExample {
    type Output = BitExample;

  fn bitand(self, other: BitExample) -> BitExample {
  match (self, other) {
  (BitExample::Yes, BitExample::Yes) => BitExample::Yes,
            (BitExample::No, BitExample::Yes) => BitExample::No,
            (BitExample::Yes, BitExample::No) => BitExample::No,
            (BitExample::No, BitExample::No) => BitExample::No,
        }
    }
}
```

BitAndAssign

The `BitAndAssign` trait enables the `&=` operator for data types that implement it.

Implementing `BitAndAssign` looks like this:

```
pub enum BitExample {
 Yes,
 No,
}

impl BitAndAssign for BitExample {
    fn bitand_assign(&mut self, other: BitExample) {
        *self = match (&self, other) {
            (BitExample::Yes, BitExample::Yes) => BitExample::Yes,
            (BitExample::No, BitExample::Yes) => BitExample::No,
            (BitExample::Yes, BitExample::No) => BitExample::No,
```

```
            (BitExample::No, BitExample::No) => BitExample::No,
        };
    }
}
```

BitOr

The `BitOr` trait enables the `|` operator for types that implement it. This operator is used for computing the *bitwise or* value of two integers, but has different meanings for various other data types.

Implementing `BitOr` looks like this:

```
pub enum BitExample {
    Yes,
    No,
}
impl BitOr for BitExample {
 type Output = BitExample;

 fn bitor(self, other: BitExample) -> BitExample {
        match (self, other) {
            (BitExample::Yes, BitExample::Yes) => BitExample::Yes,
            (BitExample::No, BitExample::Yes) => BitExample::Yes,
            (BitExample::Yes, BitExample::No) => BitExample::Yes,
            (BitExample::No, BitExample::No) => BitExample::No,
        }
    }
}
```

BitOrAssign

The `BitOrAssign` trait enables the `|=` operator for data types that implement it.

Implementing `BitOrAssign` looks like this:

```
pub enum BitExample {
 Yes,
 No,
}

impl BitOrAssign for BitExample {
    fn bitor_assign(&mut self, other: BitExample) {
        *self = match (&self, other) {
```

```
                    (BitExample::Yes, BitExample::Yes) => BitExample::Yes,
                    (BitExample::No, BitExample::Yes) => BitExample::Yes,
                    (BitExample::Yes, BitExample::No) => BitExample::Yes,
                    (BitExample::No, BitExample::No) => BitExample::No,
            };
    }
}
```

BitXor

The `BitXor` trait enables the ^ operator for types that implement it. This operator is used for computing the *bitwise exclusive or* value of two integers, but has different meanings for various other data types.

Implementing `BitXor` looks like this:

```
pub enum BitExample {
    Yes,
    No,
}

impl BitXor for BitExample {
 type Output = BitExample;

    fn bitxor(self, other: BitExample) -> BitExample {
        match (self, other) {
            (BitExample::Yes, BitExample::Yes) => BitExample::No,
            (BitExample::No, BitExample::Yes) => BitExample::Yes,
            (BitExample::Yes, BitExample::No) => BitExample::Yes,
            (BitExample::No, BitExample::No) => BitExample::No,
        }
    }
}
```

BitXorAssign

The `BitXorAssign` trait enables the ^= operator for data types that implement it.

Implementing `BitXorAssign` looks like this:

```
pub enum BitExample {
 Yes,
 No,
}
```

```
impl BitXorAssign for BitExample {
    fn bitxor_assign(&mut self, other: BitExample) {
        *self = match (&self, other) {
            (BitExample::Yes, BitExample::Yes) => BitExample::No,
            (BitExample::No, BitExample::Yes) => BitExample::Yes,
            (BitExample::Yes, BitExample::No) => BitExample::Yes,
            (BitExample::No, BitExample::No) => BitExample::No,
        };
    }
}
```

Deref

The `Deref` trait grants the ability to dereference a value as if it were a borrow. Smart pointers implement this trait, which is why they can be used as though they were borrows of the contained data value. `String` does the same thing, which is what allows us to use a `String` value anywhere that an `&str` is expected.

Here we have an implementation of the `Deref` trait:

```
pub struct DerefExample {
 val: u32,
}

impl Deref for DerefExample {
    type Target = u32;

    fn deref(&self) -> &u32 {
        return &self.val;
    }
}
```

Notice that the implementation function doesn't actually dereference anything. Instead, it converts an `&self` borrow into a borrow of something else.

That's what the compiler needs in order to correctly and efficiently handle dereferencing smart pointers and such, but the compiler also uses that ability to let us interact with something like a `Rc<Box<String>>` as if it were just a plain old `&str`. The `Rc` has a `deref` function that returns a borrow of a `Box`, and the `Box` has a `deref` function that returns a borrow of a `String`, and the `String` has a `deref` function that returns a borrow of a `str`, so the compiler lets us treat the whole thing as if it was an `&str` for the purposes of calling its functions or using it as a parameter.

DerefMut

The `DerefMut` trait does the same thing `Deref` does, but it is used when derefencing a mutable value. The compiler decides whether to use `Deref` or `DerefMut`, so usually when we need to implement one, we need to implement them both.

Here we have an implementation of `DerefMut`:

```
pub struct DerefExample {
    val: u32,
}

impl DerefMut for DerefExample {
    fn deref_mut(&mut self) -> &mut u32 {
        return &mut self.val;
    }
}
```

The `DerefMut` trait requires that the `Deref` trait is also implemented, and that the `deref` and `deref_mut` functions have the same return type.

Drop

When a data type has the `Drop` trait, the program will call the `drop` function for values of that type immediately before their lifetimes end. That's how `Rc`, `Mutex`, `RefCell`, and so on are able to keep track of how many borrows their contained value has.

The `drop` function is called before the data value's lifetime ends, so we don't have to worry about it being an invalid reference. Also, we don't have to worry about manually cleaning up the contained values for our data type, because they will be automatically dropped themselves after our `drop` function is finished. All we need to do is handle whatever special case led us to implement `Drop` in the first place.

We can't directly call the `drop` function, because that would be an extremely good way to make a mess. There is a `std::mem::drop` function we can use that consumes a data value and drops it for us, if we need to trigger this at a specific time.

Implementing `Drop` looks like this:

```
pub enum DropExample {
 Good,
 Bad,
 }
```

```
impl Drop for DropExample {
    fn drop(&mut self) {
        match self {
            DropExample::Good => println!("Good DropExample dropped"),
            DropExample::Bad => println!("Bad DropExample dropped"),
        };
    }
}
```

Index

The `Index` trait means that the data type can be used with the x[y] syntax, where a value is looked up inside of x based on the *index value* y.

When we implement `Index`, we need to identify what data type can be used for the index value, as well as what data type the operation returns, so the implementation looks like this:

```
pub struct IndexExample {
    first: u32,
    second: u32,
    third: u32,
}

impl<'a> Index<&'a str> for IndexExample {
    type Output = u32;

    fn index(&self, index: &'a str) -> &u32 {
        match index {
            "first" => &self.first,
            "second" => &self.second,
            "third" => &self.third,
            _ => &0,
        }
    }
}
```

We've used &str for the data type of the index, and were using u32 for the data type of the value. Using &str means that we need to be a little bit careful of lifetimes, but it's not too bad.

IndexMut

The `IndexMut` trait represents the abilities to assign to a contained value using the `x[y]` = z syntax. Like the `Index` trait, it lets us look up a contained data value by providing an index value, but it produces a mutable borrow of the contained value, which can be used to change it.

Implementing `IndexMut` looks like this:

```
pub struct IndexExample {
  first: u32,
  second: u32,
  third: u32,
  junk: u32,
}

impl<'a> IndexMut<&'a str> for IndexExample {
    fn index_mut(&mut self, index: &'a str) -> &mut u32 {
        match index {
            "first" => &mut self.first,
            "second" => &mut self.second,
            "third" => &mut self.third,
            _ => &mut self.junk,
        }
    }
}
```

Notice that we've added a `junk` value to the `IndexExample` structure. We did that because there's no way to indicate that an index value doesn't map to a valid contained value; if the `index_mut` function gets called, is *has* to return a mutable borrow of the correct type, and that borrow has to have a long enough lifetime as well. Adding a junk value to the data structure is a simple way of achieving that, though there are other approaches that would save memory.

Any type that implements `IndexMut` has to implement `Index` as well, and the `index` and `index_mut` functions have to return a borrow and a mutable borrow of the same data type, respectively.

Neg

The `Neg` trait enables a data type to be used with the *unary negation* operator, also known as the negative sign. When we write −5, we're applying the unary negation operator to the value 5, producing a negative 5 as the result.

Implementing `Neg` looks like this:

```
pub enum NegExample {
 Yes,
 No,
}

impl Neg for NegExample {
 type Output = NegExample;

 fn neg(self) -> NegExample {
 match self {
 NegExample::Yes => NegExample::No,
 NegExample::No => NegExample::Yes,
 }
 }
}
```

Not

The `Not` trait enables the *logical negation* operator, which is written as an `!`. `Not` is both conceptually and practically similar to `Neg`, but its primary use is for Boolean logic rather than arithmetic.

Implementing `Not` looks like this:

```
pub enum NotExample {
 True,
 False,
}

impl Not for NotExample {
    type Output = NotExample;

    fn not(self) -> NotExample {
        match self {
            NotExample::True => NotExample::False,
            NotExample::False => NotExample::True,
        }
    }
}
```

Rem and RemAssign

The `Rem` trait enables the `%` operator for types that implement it. This operator is used for computing the *modulus* (also known as the remainder of a division) value of two integers, but has different meanings for various other data types.

The `Rem` trait has both an `Output` associated type, and the option of implementing it to operate on different types by implementing `Rem<OtherType>` rather than just `Rem`.

`RemAssign` has the same relationship to `Rem` that `AddAssign` has to `Add`.

Shl and ShlAssign

The `Shl` trait enables the `<<` operator for types that implement it. This operator is used for *left-shifting* an integer by a number of bits, but has different meanings for various other data types.

The `Shl` trait has both an output associated type, and the option of implementing it to operate on different types by implementing `Shl<OtherType>` rather than just `Shl`.

`ShlAssign` has the same relationship to `Shl` that `AddAssign` has to `Add`.

Shr and ShrAssign

The `Shr` trait enables the `>>` operator for types that implement it. This operator is used for *right-shifting* an integer by a number of bits, but has different meanings for various other data types.

The `Shr` trait has both an `Output` associated type, and the option of implementing it to operate on different types by implementing `Shr<OtherType>` rather than just `Shr`.

`ShrAssign` has the same relationship to `Shr` that `AddAssign` has to `Add`.

Traits that are implemented automatically

There are a few traits that are automatically implemented where appropriate, without even a `#[derive()]` tag. These tend to represent extremely low-level aspects of the data types in question.

Sync

The Sync trait is automatically applied to any data type that can safely be borrowed between threads.

While our data types will have the Sync trait automatically if they qualify for it, occasionally we want to be sure that a data type *does not* have Sync, even if it looks to the compiler like it should.

We can achieve that by implementing !Sync for our data type:

```
pub enum NotSyncExample {
  Good,
  Bad,
}

impl !Sync for NotSyncExample {}
```

We don't actually need any functions inside of !Sync. All we're doing is telling the compiler that the Sync trait is inappropriate for this type.

As of Rust 1.29, implementing !Sync is still considered an unstable feature, and is not available in the stable build of the compiler. It can be enabled in the nightly build by placing #![feature(optin_builtin_traits)] at the top of the file.

A lot of data types have the Sync trait, but Rc, Cell, and RefCell are notable examples of types that do not. Arc, Mutex, and RwLock do, though.

Send

The Send trait is automatically applied to any data type that can safely be moved between threads. It is a close relative of Sync, and like Sync, we can implement !Send to tell the compiler that a data type should *not* have the trait.

If we don't explicitly forbid it, the compiler decides whether a type has the Send trait based on whether the types it contains have the trait.

Sized

The Sized trait is automatically applied to any data type for which the size is known by the compiler. All trait bounds automatically include Sized as an additional, implicit requirement, unless we instead tell it that ?Sized is the requirement. If we explicitly declare a trait bound is ?Sized, that means that the data type that matches the bound is allowed to be Sized, but not required.

Fn

The Fn trait is automatically applied to any function or closure that uses only immutable borrows to access data outside its own scope.

This is a strict requirement, and many functions and closures fail that test, so Fn is the least common of the function traits.

FnMut

The FnMut trait is automatically applied to any function or closure that uses mutable or immutable borrows to access data outside its own scope.

This is a moderate requirement, but some functions and closures fail that test, so FnMut is more common than Fn.

FnOnce

The FnOnce trait is automatically applied to any function that uses mutable borrows, immutable borrows, or moved variables to access data outside its own scope.

The is a loose requirement, which any function or closure will satisfy, so FnOnce is the most common of the function traits.

Summary

In this chapter, we have done the following:

- Looked at many different traits
- Examined the traits' specific meanings and how they interact with syntax of Rust
- Learned about the details of implementing the traits
- Learned how to easily derive traits that support that feature

We've reached the end of this quick start guide, but the journey is never over. Good luck on your next steps.

Other Books You May Enjoy

If you enjoyed this book, you may be interested in these other books by Packt:

Rust Standard Library Cookbook
Jan Nils Ferner, Daniel Durante

ISBN: 978-1-78862-392-6

- How to use the basic modules of the library: strings, command line access, and more
- Implement collections and folding of collections using vectors, Deque, linked lists, and more
- Handle various file types , compressing and decompressing data
  Search for files with glob patterns
- Implement parsing through various formats such as CSV, TOML, and JSON
- Utilize drop trait , the Rust version of destructor
- Resource locking with Bilocks

Hands-On Concurrency with Rust
Brian L. Troutwine

ISBN: 978-1-78839-997-5

- Probe your programs for performance and accuracy issues
- Create your own threading and multi-processing environment in Rust
- Use coarse locks from Rust's Standard library
- Solve common synchronization problems or avoid synchronization using atomic programming
- Build lock-free/wait-free structures in Rust and understand their implementations in the crates ecosystem
- Leverage Rust's memory model and type system to build safety properties into your parallel programs
- Understand the new features of the Rust programming language to ease the writing of parallel programs

Leave a review - let other readers know what you think

Please share your thoughts on this book with others by leaving a review on the site that you bought it from. If you purchased the book from Amazon, please leave us an honest review on this book's Amazon page. This is vital so that other potential readers can see and use your unbiased opinion to make purchasing decisions, we can understand what our customers think about our products, and our authors can see your feedback on the title that they have worked with Packt to create. It will only take a few minutes of your time, but is valuable to other potential customers, our authors, and Packt. Thank you!

Index